THE CLASSIC AMERICAN
QUILT COLLECTION™
◇
BASKETS

Volume Editors

Mary V. Green and Karen Costello Soltys

 Rodale Press, Emmaus, Pennsylvania

Our Mission

We publish books that empower people's lives.

RODALE BOOKS

THE CLASSIC AMERICAN QUILT COLLECTION: BASKETS EDITORIAL AND DESIGN STAFF

Volume Editors:
Mary V. Green and Karen Costello Soltys

Technical Writer: Janet Wickell

Quilt Scout: Bettina Havig

Cover and Interior Designer: Denise M. Shade

Book Layout: Carol Angstadt and Lisa Palmer

Cover Photographer: Mitch Mandel

Interior Photographers: Mitch Mandel and Kurt Wilson

Illustrators: Mario Ferro and Jackie Walsh

Technical Artist: Tanya L. Lipinski

Copy Editor: Carolyn Mandarano

Administrative Assistant: Susan Nickol

Production Coordinator: Jodi Schaffer

RODALE BOOKS

Executive Editor, Home and Garden: Margaret Lydic Balitas

Managing Editor, Quilt Books: Suzanne Nelson

Art Director, Home and Garden: Michael Mandarano

Copy Manager, Home and Garden: Dolores Plikaitis

Office Manager, Home and Garden: Karen Earl-Braymer

Editor-in-Chief: William Gottlieb

If you have any questions or comments concerning this book, please write to:
Rodale Press, Inc.
Book Readers' Service
33 East Minor Street
Emmaus, PA 18098

The photo of Amish Easter Baskets on page 34 appears courtesy of the Collection of the Museum of the American Quilter's Society, Paducah, Ky. Photo: DSI Studios, Evansville, Ind.

Library of Congress Cataloging-in-Publication Data

The classic American quilt collection. Baskets /
   volume editors, Mary V. Green and Karen Costello
   Soltys.
      p. cm.
   ISBN 0–87596–644–6 hardcover
   1. Patchwork—Patterns. 2. Quilting—Patterns.
   3. Baskets in art. I. Green, Mary V. II. Soltys, Karen
Costello. III. Rodale Press.
TT835.C577   1994
746.46—dc20   94–30877
                                                CIP

Distributed in the book trade by St. Martin's Press

2 4 6 8 10 9 7 5 3   hardcover

CONTENTS

Acknowledgments

Fruit Baskets, owned by Cindy Rennels, Clinton, Oklahoma. The proprietor of Cindy's Quilts in Clinton, Oklahoma, Cindy has been collecting and dealing with antique quilts for the past eight years.

Postage Stamp Baskets, hand pieced and hand quilted by Martha Bastian, Mexico, Missouri. Martha is a member of the Prairie Pine Quilt Guild and considers herself lucky to have a husband who shares her enthusiasm for quilting and compliments her on her quilts.

Red-and-Orange Baskets, owned by Irene Metz, Harleysville, Pennsylvania. This quilt was made by Katie Young, believed to be Irene's great-aunt, around the turn of the century. Katie was from Montgomery County, Pennsylvania, an area known for Mennonite quilters.

Bluebirds of Happiness, owned by Marian Costello Mongelli, Norristown, Pennsylvania. This quilt was made by either Marian's grandmother or great-aunt in the 1920s or 1930s, but the exact date and maker remain unknown. Marian, a clothing designer and seamstress by trade, appreciates the beauty and value of quilts and is happy to own several antique quilts made by family members.

Amish Easter Baskets, made by Elsie Vredenburg, Tustin, Michigan. Amish Easter Baskets has been judged at numerous quilt shows and has won awards totaling $2,700. Elsie donated this beauty to the Museum of the American Quilter's Society (MAQS) in Paducah, Kentucky. The quilt appears here courtesy of Elsie and MAQS. Elsie is an accomplished quilter who drafted the pattern for Amish Easter Baskets based on an antique quilt.

Carolina Lily Medallion, owned by Cindy Rennels, Clinton, Oklahoma, a quilt collector and dealer.

Blue-and-White Cherry Baskets, owned by Martha Bastian, Mexico, Missouri. This quilt was made by Martha's grandmother, Susan Boyd, of Paris, Missouri, in the 1920s. Martha has been quilting since 1986 and has gained a lot of inspiration from her grandmother's quilts. Like her grandmother, Martha enjoys making quilts entirely by hand, including piecing, appliquéing, and quilting.

Scrap Baskets with Nine-Patch Sashing, by Wilma Sestric, Ballwin, Missouri. Wilma started out as a painter, teaching tole and decorative painting to students at her art shop. She turned to quiltmaking 12 years ago and just loves the creative outlet it provides.

Red-and-Green Appliquéd Baskets, owned by Cindy Rennels, Clinton, Oklahoma. This quilt is believed to have been made between 1860 and 1870 in the northeastern United States.

Amish-Style Scrap Baskets, pieced by Naoko Anne Ito, Berkeley, California, and quilted by Betty Schoenhals. Naoko Anne drafted the pattern herself and machine pieced the quilt top. It wasn't until eight years later that she found Betty, a quilter she trusted to do the fine hand quilting. Naoko Anne is a member of the East Bay Heritage Quilters and has organized the first United States/Japan quilting symposium. She has also taken several groups of American quilters and teachers to Japan.

Antique Lily Baskets, owned by Joan Townsend. Joan is the proprietor of Oh Suzanna, an antique linens and quilt shop in Lebanon, Ohio, which has been established for 15 years. This quilt is from Indiana, and it dates back to the 1880s.

Flower Baskets, owned by Cindy Rennels, Clinton, Oklahoma, a quilt collector and dealer.

INTRODUCTION

No quilt collection of our grandmother's day was complete without a basket quilt.
—Carrie A. Hall, 1935

Sixty years ago, the basket quilt was already considered a classic. Even today, poised on the brink of the twenty-first century, quiltmakers still love this simple motif with its country-style charm. A quick glimpse at the history of basket quilts reveals why they've remained so well loved.

Baskets were one of the first realistic motifs used by American quiltmakers. Their history can be traced back to the mid-nineteenth century, when *broderie perse* was popular. Baskets, urns, and vases were cut from printed chintzes and appliquéd onto quilt tops to achieve a realistic-looking design.

Although that style of appliqué declined in favor, the idea of using baskets and their close relatives remained popular. In the mid-1800s, around the time that the all-American classic, the Log Cabin, was gaining popularity, artful quilters were also beginning to incorporate pieced basket blocks in their quilting. Baskets even enjoyed a revival in the 1920s and 1930s, when quiltmaking in general was going through a resurgence.

Perhaps one reason why baskets have remained such cherished motifs in quiltmaking is that they offer ample opportunity for creativity. They can be filled with flowers and fruit and be pieced or appliquéd. They can be set on point or used as central medallions. And they can be as realistic or as impressionistic as a quiltmaker desires. In short, basket quilts offer no limits on imagination and personal style.

Just looking at the many names and adaptations developed over the history of American quiltmaking gives the sense that quiltmakers have enjoyed making and creating new basket quilts for more than 125 years. The basket was a well-used tool of the early American home and was given a place of honor in many shapes and forms on the American

quilt, from May Baskets to Fruit Baskets, Flower Baskets to Cactus Baskets, and Grape Baskets to Cherry Baskets.

In this volume, you'll find several examples of antique basket quilts, both appliquéd and pieced. The oldest quilt in this collection, the Red-and-Green Appliquéd Baskets on page 68, dates back to the 1860s. You'll find a few other quilts from the nineteenth century, too.

We've also gathered several delightful quilts from the 1920s through 1930s basket-revival era. Blue-and-White Cherry Baskets (page 52), Flower Baskets (page 96), and Bluebirds of Happiness (page 24) each have a soft, lighthearted, romantic feel. Perhaps quiltmakers turned to gaily colored pastel prints and solid fabrics for encouragement and cheer during that time of financial woes.

As you turn the pages, you will also find a sampling of delightful modern-day quilts, proving that the basket theme is still going strong. There's no great mystery why some of these basket quilts were made entirely of scraps. What quilter doesn't have leftover bits of fabric just waiting to be cut into little triangles to form the baskets? Postage Stamp Baskets on page 8 and Scrap Baskets with Nine-Patch Sashing on page 60 are two wonderful and inspirational examples of scrap basket quilts.

Whatever styles you prefer, our hope is that you will use this book to explore the versatility of the time-honored basket quilt. Use it to re-create a family heirloom or as inspiration for your own creative quiltmaking ideas.

Karen Soltys

Karen Costello Soltys

BASKET ◇ PROJECTS

FRUIT BASKETS

Skill Level: *Easy*

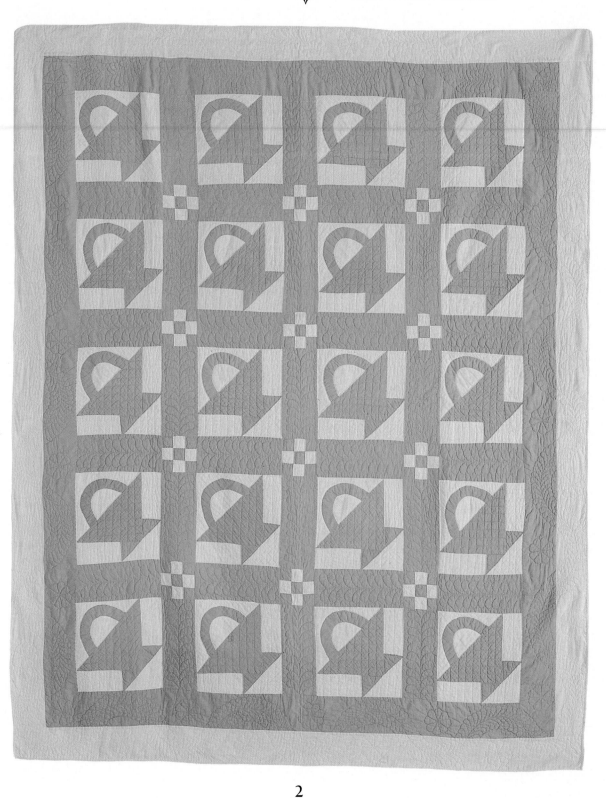

*T*he easy construction and sweet but simple color scheme make this a good quilt for a beginner. This twin-size quilt was obtained from an estate in Thomas, Oklahoma. Its pattern and colors indicate that it was probably made in the 1930s, a time of great quilting activity.

BEFORE YOU BEGIN

The directions for this quilt are based on using rotary-cutting techniques. The pieces for the Fruit Basket blocks can be cut from strips; the triangles are simply squares cut in half. The handles are bias-cut strips appliquéd in place. For the Nine-Patch blocks, strips of fabric are sewn into strip sets, which are cut apart and resewn into blocks.

CHOOSING FABRICS

Part of this quilt's charm lies in the simplicity of its color scheme. For a different look, try using several different solids or mix and match solid and print blocks.

To help you develop your own unique color scheme for the quilt, photocopy the **Color Plan** on page 7, and use crayons or colored pencils to experiment with different color arrangements.

CUTTING

All measurements include ¼-inch seam allowances. Referring to the Cutting Chart, cut the required number of strips in the width needed. Except for the bias strips for the basket handles, cut all strips across the fabric width. When you have cut the number of strips listed in the Cutting Chart, refer to the instructions here to cut the individual pieces.

• For the large pink triangles, cut the 8⅜-inch-wide strips into 8⅜-inch squares. Cut each square in half diagonally, as shown in **Diagram 1** on page 4.

• For the triangles for the base of the basket, cut the 3⅜-inch-wide pink strips into 3⅜-inch squares. Cut each square in half diagonally.

Quilt Sizes		
	Twin (shown)	Double
Finished Quilt Size	70" × 84½"	99" × 84½"
Finished Block Size		
Fruit Basket	10"	10"
Nine Patch	4½"	4½"
Number of Blocks		
Fruit Basket	20	30
Nine Patch	12	20

Materials		
	Twin	Double
Pink	3¾ yards	5¼ yards
Muslin	2¾ yards	3¾ yards
Backing	5¼ yards	8 yards
Batting	76" × 90"	90" × 105"
Binding	⅝ yard	¾ yard

NOTE: *Yardages are based on 44/45-inch-wide fabrics that are at least 42 inches wide after preshrinking.*

3

Cutting Chart

Fabric	Used For	Strip Width	Number to Cut	
			Twin	Double
Pink	Basket blocks	8⅜"	2	3
	Basket blocks	3⅜"	2	3
	Sashing strips	5"	8	13
	Inner border	5"	7	9
	Nine-Patch blocks	2"	5	5
Muslin	Basket blocks	8⅜"	2	3
	Basket blocks	5⅞"	2	3
	Basket blocks	3"	6	9
	Outer border	4¼"	7	9
	Nine-Patch blocks	2"	4	4

• For the basket handles, cut 1¾ × 10¾-inch bias strips of pink fabric. Refer to page 110 in "Basket Basics" for details on cutting bias strips.

• For the sashing strips, cut the 5-inch-wide pink strips into 5 × 10½-inch rectangles.

• For the large muslin triangles, cut the 8⅜-inch-wide strips into 8⅜-inch squares, then cut each square in half diagonally.

• For the bottom of the baskets, cut the 5⅞-inch muslin strips into 5⅞-inch squares. Cut the squares in half diagonally.

• For the sides of the baskets, cut the 3-inch-wide muslin strips into 3 × 5½-inch rectangles.

Note: Cut and piece one sample block before cutting all the fabric for the quilt.

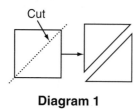

Diagram 1

PIECING THE BLOCKS

The Fruit Basket blocks consist of a simple pieced basket with an appliquéd handle. Nine-Patch blocks form the cornerstones of the sashing. Both blocks are illustrated in the **Block Diagram**.

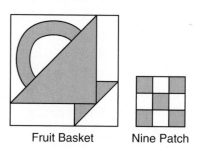

Fruit Basket   Nine Patch

Block Diagram

Making the Basket Blocks

Step 1. For one Fruit Basket block, assemble one large pink triangle, two small pink triangles, one large muslin triangle, one small muslin triangle, and two 3 × 5½-inch muslin rectangles.

Step 2. Sew a small pink triangle to the end of two 3 × 5½-inch rectangles. See **Diagram 2** for position. Press the seams toward the triangles.

Step 3. Referring to **Diagram 3**, sew a Step 2 unit to each side of the large pink triangle. Press the seams toward the pink triangle.

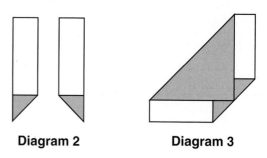

Diagram 2   **Diagram 3**

Step 4. Fold a small muslin triangle in half to find the midpoint of its longest side. Sew the triangle to the base of the basket, aligning the fold with the point of the large pink triangle. Press the seam toward the muslin triangle.

Step 5. The basket handle will be appliquéd to the large muslin triangle. Refer to page 110 in "Basket Basics" to prepare the handle. To position the handle on the triangle, fold the triangle in half and lightly crease it. Fold the bias handle strip in half crosswise and crease. Refer to **Diagram 4** to position the handle on the triangle, using the dimensions as placement guidelines. Trim the ends of the strip so they are flush with the edge of the triangle. Baste the handle in position.

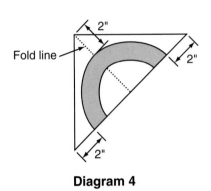

Diagram 4

Step 6. Using a ¼-inch seam, sew the muslin triangle with the handle to the basket portion of the block. Appliqué the handle in place.

Step 7. Repeat Steps 1 through 6 to make the number of Fruit Basket blocks required for your quilt.

Making the Nine-Patch Blocks

The Nine-Patch blocks can be quickly assembled using strip-piecing techniques.

Step 1. Sew a 2-inch-wide pink strip to either side of a 2-inch muslin strip, as shown in **Diagram 5**. Press the seams toward the pink strips. Using a rotary cutter and ruler, square up one end of the strip set, then cut as many 2-inch-wide segments from it as possible.

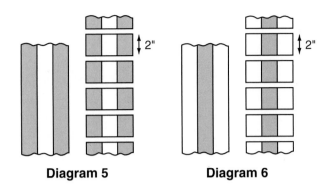

Diagram 5   **Diagram 6**

Step 2. Sew a 2-inch-wide muslin strip to either side of a 2-inch-wide pink strip (see **Diagram 6**). Press the seams toward the pink strip. Cut it into 2-inch-wide segments as you did in Step 1.

Step 3. Referring to the **Block Diagram,** sew a Step 1 segment to each side of a Step 2 segment, matching seams. Press the seams to one side.

Step 4. Repeat Steps 1 through 3 to make the number of Nine-Patch blocks required for your quilt.

ASSEMBLING THE QUILT TOP

Step 1. Lay out the Fruit Basket blocks, Nine-Patch blocks, and 5 × 10½-inch pink sashing strips, referring to the **Quilt Diagram** on page 6. The twin-size quilt is shown. The double size will have five vertical rows with six blocks per row.

Step 2. Sew the blocks and sashing strips into rows, as shown. Press the seams toward the pink rectangles. Sew the rows together, matching seams.

ADDING THE BORDERS

Step 1. For the twin-size quilt, sew together two pink strips each for the side borders and one and a half strips each for the top and bottom borders. For the double size, sew together two and a half pink strips each for the side borders and two strips each for the top and bottom borders.

Step 2. Measure the width of your quilt through the center rather than along the edges. Trim the top and bottom border strips to this length. Fold one strip in half crosswise and crease. Unfold it and position it right side down along one end of the quilt, with the crease at the vertical midpoint. Pin at the midpoint and ends first, then across the width of the quilt, easing in fullness if necessary. Sew the border to the quilt. Repeat on the opposite end of the quilt.

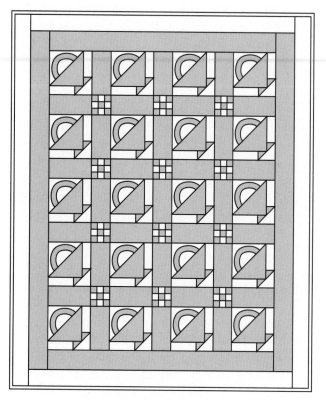

Quilt Diagram

Step 3. Measure the length of the quilt through the center, including the top and bottom borders. Trim the side borders to this length. Position and pin the side borders as you did for the top and bottom borders. Stitch, easing in fullness if necessary.

Step 4. To add the outer border, piece the muslin strips to make four long borders. For the twin-size quilt, sew two muslin strips together for each side border and one and a half strips for the top and bottom borders. For the double-size quilt, sew two and a half muslin strips together for each side border and two strips for the top and bottom borders.

Step 5. Measure and add the outer borders as described for the pink borders.

QUILTING AND FINISHING

Step 1. Mark the top for quilting. The quilt shown has cross-hatching in the lower half of the baskets and feathers quilted in the sashing and borders. The Nine-Patch blocks were outline quilted.

Step 2. Regardless of which quilt size you've chosen to make, the backing will have to be pieced, as shown in **Diagram 7.** To make the backing for the twin size, cut the fabric in half crosswise, and trim the selvages. Cut one piece in half lengthwise, and sew one half to each side of the full-width piece. Press the seams open.

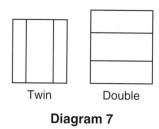

Twin   Double

Diagram 7

Step 3. For the double-size quilt, cut the backing fabric into three equal pieces, and trim the selvages. Sew the three segments together along the long sides, and press the seams open.

Step 4. Layer the backing, batting, and quilt top, and baste. Quilt as desired.

Step 5. Referring to page 121 in "Quiltmaking Basics," make and attach double-fold binding. Add the length of the four sides of the quilt plus 9 inches to calculate the amount of binding you will need.

FRUIT BASKETS
Color Plan

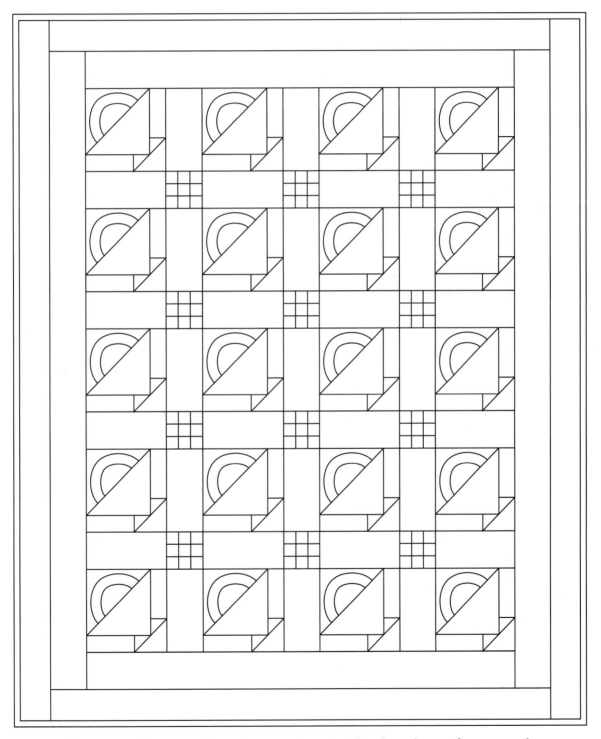

Photocopy this page and use it to experiment with color schemes for your quilt.

POSTAGE STAMP BASKETS
Skill Level: *Easy*

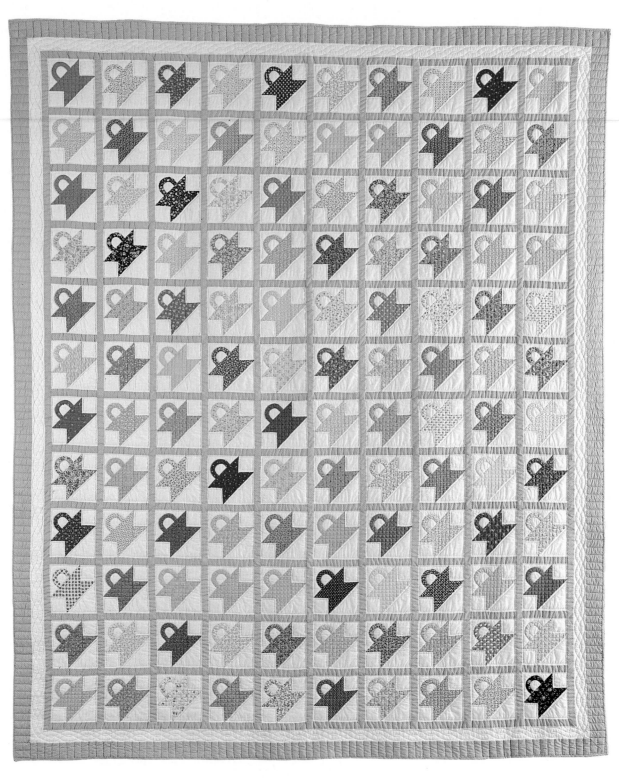

hese little baskets are a delightful way to use leftover bits of fabric from your scrap bag. A quick-and-easy project that's perfectly suited to beginners, this petite basket was named the May Basket by the Kansas City Star *in 1941. Today, it is often called the Postage Stamp Basket, since it appeared on a U.S. commemorative stamp issued in 1978. The queen-size quilt in the photograph was made in the 1990s, so we've decided to use the modern name, too.*

BEFORE YOU BEGIN

The directions for this quilt are written based on rotary cutting and quick piecing. Unlike many of the pieced baskets in this book, the Postage Stamp Baskets are made of just one large triangle with two smaller triangles forming the feet. The basket handle is appliquéd from bias-cut strips, so no templates are required for this project.

CHOOSING FABRICS

The maker of the quilt pictured stitched the quilt specifically to use her many scraps saved over the years from her daughters' dresses. If you're a beginner quiltmaker and haven't accumulated a large quantity of scraps yet, you can still achieve the scrappy look by purchasing small amounts of lots of fabrics you like. Take advantage of the many fat quarters and fat eighths that are common in quilt shops now. Or swap and trade with friends or guild members.

The goal is not to match or coordinate too precisely. For a sparkling scrap quilt, use many different colors, prints, and values in your baskets. They will be unified with the white background and a single-color sashing.

If you prefer a less random look, use the **Color Plan** on page 15 to determine the color choices that are right for you. Make several photocopies of the **Color Plan**, and use crayons or markers to experiment with different color arrangements.

Quilt Sizes		
	Crib	Queen (shown)
Finished Quilt Size	45½" × 59½"	80½" × 94½"
Finished Block Size	6"	6"
Number of Blocks	35	120

Materials		
	Crib	Queen
Assorted prints	18 fat eighths or scraps totaling 2½ yards	60 fat eighths or scraps totaling 7¾ yards
White	1⅝ yards	4 yards
Green print	1½ yards	3 yards
Backing	3 yards	7¾ yards
Batting	52" × 66"	88" × 101"
Binding	½ yard	¾ yard

NOTE: Yardages are based on 44/45-inch-wide fabrics that are at least 42 inches wide after preshrinking.

9

Cutting Chart

Fabric	Used For	Strip Width	Number of Strips	
			Crib	Queen
Assorted prints	Baskets	4⁷/₈"	3*	8*
	Basket feet	2⁷/₈"	3*	9*
White	Basket background	4⁷/₈"	5	15
	Basket background	2¹/₂"	5	15
	Middle border	2¹/₂"	6	10
Green print	Sashing strips	1¹/₂"	10	35
	Inner border	1¹/₂"	6	10
	Outer border	3"	6	10

*NOTE: *The number of strips to cut assumes you are cutting from 42-inch-wide fabric. If you are using fat eighths or fat quarters, double the number of strips to cut.*

CUTTING

All measurements include ¹/₄-inch seam allowances. Referring to the Cutting Chart, cut the required number of strips in the width needed. Cut all strips across the fabric width (crosswise grain). When you have cut the number of strips listed in the Cutting Chart, refer to the instructions here to cut the individual pieces. Many of the squares will need to be cut in half diagonally. Refer to **Diagram 1** for this step.

• For the baskets, cut the 4⁷/₈-inch-wide assorted strips into 4⁷/₈-inch squares. Cut 18 squares for the crib-size quilt and 60 squares for the queen-size quilt. Cut the squares in half diagonally.

• For the basket feet, cut the 2⁷/₈-inch-wide assorted strips into 2⁷/₈-inch squares. You need 35 for the crib quilt and 120 for the queen size. Cut the squares in half diagonally.

• For the basket handles, refer to page 110 in "Basket Basics" for tips on cutting bias basket handles. For each basket, you need a ³/₄ × 7-inch bias strip that finishes to a ¹/₂-inch width.

• For the basket background, cut the 4⁷/₈-inch-wide white strips into squares. Cut 35 squares for the crib quilt and 120 for the queen size. Cut the squares in half diagonally.

• For the basket background, cut the 2¹/₂-inch-wide white strips into 2¹/₂-inch squares.

• For the sashing strips, cut the 1¹/₂-inch-wide green print strips into 1¹/₂ × 6¹/₂-inch rectangles. Cut 30 rectangles for the crib quilt and 110 rectangles for the queen size. Reserve the remaining green strips for making the vertical sashing.

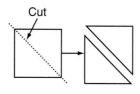

Cut

Diagram 1

PIECING THE BASKET BLOCKS

The cutting instructions will yield enough pieces from each basket fabric to make two blocks.

Note: Assemble one sample block before cutting all the pieces required for your quilt.

Step 1. To make the basket feet, sew two 2⁷/₈-inch basket fabric triangles to two 2¹/₂-inch white squares, as shown in **Diagram 2.** Press the seams toward the triangles.

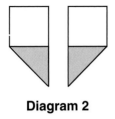

Diagram 2

Step 2. Sew the basket feet to the short sides of the large basket fabric triangle, as shown in **Diagram 3**. Press the seams toward the large triangle.

Diagram 3

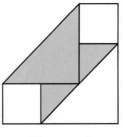

Diagram 4

Step 4. Center and appliqué a matching basket fabric handle to a $4^7/8$-inch white triangle using a blind stitch or other stitch of your choice. Then sew the white triangle to the basket, as shown in the **Block Diagram.** Press the seam toward the dark triangle.

Block Diagram

Step 5. Repeat Steps 1 through 4, making a duplicate block from the remaining basket fabric pieces. Continue making pairs of blocks from the basket fabrics in the same manner until you have assembled the total number required for your quilt (35 for the crib size or 120 for the queen size).

ASSEMBLING THE QUILT TOP

Step 1. Use a design wall or other flat surface to arrange your blocks and sashing strips, as shown in the **Assembly Diagram** on page 12. Notice that short sashing strips are used to join the blocks into vertical columns and long strips link the columns together. The diagram shows the queen-size quilt. The crib quilt should be laid out in a similar manner, with five vertical rows of seven blocks each.

Sew Easy

Squaring off the tips that extend beyond the edge of the long side of the large triangles can help you match up units more easily. Align the $4^1/2$-inch horizontal markings on a rotary ruler with the right angle of your triangle. Use your rotary cutter to trim away the triangle tip that extends beyond the edge of your ruler. Repeat for the other tip. Now your triangle and square edges will line up perfectly for easy piecing.

Step 3. Sew a $4^7/8$-inch white triangle to the bottom of the basket, as shown in **Diagram 4.** Press the seam toward the white triangle.

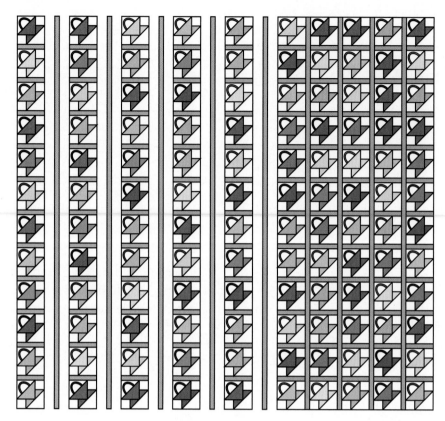

Assembly Diagram

Make a temporary design area by pinning or taping lengths of flannel side by side onto a wall. Blocks will stick to the flannel, allowing you to easily change the layout. Step back from the wall and view the arrangement from a distance. Then, turn your back to the block layout, briefly turn to view the quilt, and turn away again. What was your impression? If it didn't appeal to you, rearrange the blocks until you are satisfied with the color placement.

Step 2. Sew the blocks and short sashing strips together. Press the seams toward the sashing strips.

Step 3. Mark the long sashing strips at the seam intersections to ensure that blocks will align horizontally when columns are sewn together. Your first mark should be $6^{1}/_{4}$ inches from one end to allow for the 6-inch finished block size plus the $^{1}/_{4}$-inch seam allowance at the column's end. Since the finished width of sashing is 1 inch, your next mark will be 1 inch past the first mark. Continue, alternately marking at 6-inch then 1-inch intervals until you reach the end of the strip, as shown in **Diagram 5.** The final mark should be $6^{1}/_{4}$ inches from the end of the strip.

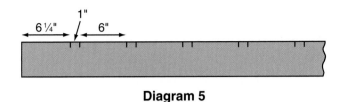

Diagram 5

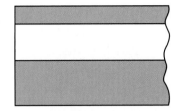

Diagram 6

Step 4. Pin and sew the long sashing strips to the columns of blocks, as shown in the **Assembly Diagram,** matching seam intersections carefully. Press the seams toward the long sashing strips.

ADDING THE MITERED BORDERS

This quilt has three borders, beginning with a narrow inner strip that matches the sashing. The center border is white, and the outer border repeats the sashing fabric. You will sew the three long strips for each side together first, then add them to the quilt top as a single unit, mitering the corners. Refer to page 119 in "Quiltmaking Basics" for complete details on adding borders with mitered corners.

Step 1. To determine the correct length for the side borders, measure the quilt top vertically through the center. To this measurement, add two times the finished width of the three borders ($5\frac{1}{2}$ inches $\times$ 2 = 11 inches), plus approximately 5 inches. This is the length you need to make the two side borders. In the same manner, measure the quilt top horizontally through the center, and calculate the length of the top and bottom borders.

Step 2. Refer to the cutting chart for the total number of border strips required for your quilt. Sew matching border strips together end to end until you've achieved the required length needed for your quilt. Be sure to keep the side border strips separate from the top and bottom border strips. **Diagram 6** illustrates the color placement of the border strips.

Step 3. Working with the side border strips first, pin and sew the long strips together lengthwise into two units. Press the seams toward the widest border.

Step 4. In the same manner, pin and sew the top and bottom border strips together into two units. Press the seams toward the innermost border.

Step 5. Pin and sew the four border units to the quilt top. Refer to page 119 in "Quiltmaking Basics" for complete instructions on adding borders with mitered corners. When preparing the miters, be sure to carefully match up like strips in adjacent borders. See the **Quilt Diagram** on page 14.

QUILTING AND FINISHING

Step 1. Mark the quilt top for quilting, if desired. The quilt shown was quilted in the ditch.

Step 2. Regardless of which quilt size you've chosen to make, the backing will have to be pieced. **Diagram 7** shows the layout for both quilt

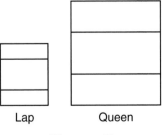

Lap   Queen

Diagram 7

backs. For the crib quilt, divide the backing fabric crosswise into two equal pieces, and trim the selvages. Trim two 14-inch widths from one segment, then sew one narrow segment to each side of the full-width piece. Press the seams open.

Step 3. For the queen-size quilt, divide the backing fabric crosswise into three equal pieces, and trim the selvages. Trim a 31-inch width from two segments, then sew one narrow segment to each side of the full-width piece, as shown.

Step 4. Layer the quilt top, batting, and backing, and baste the layers together. Quilt as desired.

Step 5. Referring to the directions on page 121 in "Quiltmaking Basics," make and attach double-fold binding. To calculate the amount of binding needed for the quilt size you are making, add the length of the four sides plus 9 inches. The total is the approximate number of inches of binding you will need.

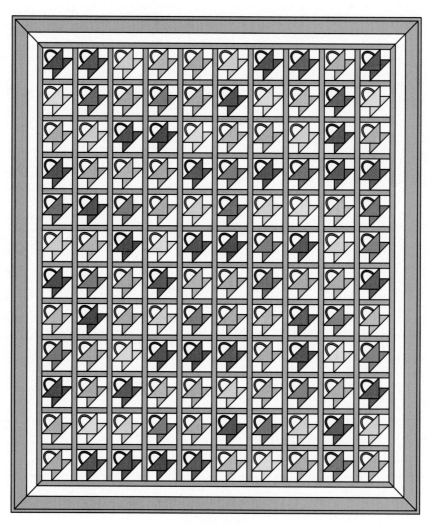

Quilt Diagram

Postage Stamp Baskets
Color Plan

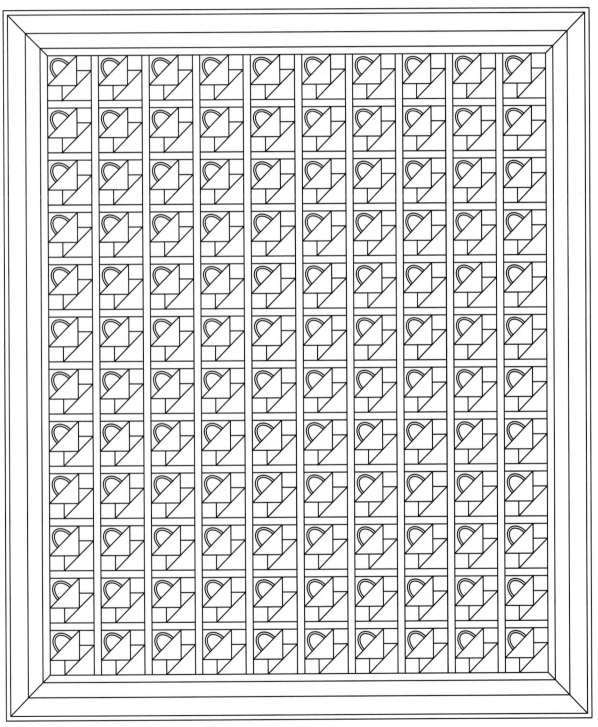

Photocopy this page and use it to experiment with color schemes for your quilt.

RED-AND-ORANGE BASKETS

Skill Level: *Intermediate*

This well-preserved quilt was made by Katie Young of Franconia Township in Pennsylvania around the turn of the century. Although Katie died at an early age, the quilt has remained in her family for three generations. It is a delightful example of the deep turkey red and bright cheddar orange shades used so often in combination with dark green by Mennonite quilters. Katie pieced this quilt entirely by machine, including the appliquéd basket handles. The quilting, however, was hand stitched in black.

BEFORE YOU BEGIN

We have changed the basket base slightly for these instructions to avoid templates and set-in seams. Because this quilt is pieced from a large number of triangle squares, we recommend using the grid method for piecing. This method is both easy and accurate. You'll find complete instructions on using this method on page 106 in "Basket Basics."

Before appliquéing the handles of your baskets, read through the information on various appliqué techniques on page 108 in "Basket Basics."

CHOOSING FABRICS

The colors of this quilt are very representative of Mennonite quilts—deep, rich, solid hues. To achieve the same look for your quilt, select similar shades of red, green, and orange. Or select a color combination all your own. The baskets would look just as nice in print fabrics or even in a variety of scrap fabrics. To help develop your own unique color scheme for the quilt, photocopy the **Color Plan** on page 23, and use crayons or colored pencils to experiment with different color arrangements.

Quilt Sizes		
	Twin (shown)	Queen
Finished Quilt Size	77½" × 85¼"	93" × 108½"
Finished Block Size	9"	9"
Number of Basket Blocks	45	71

Materials		
	Twin	Queen
Red	3½ yards	5¼ yards
Orange	1⅛ yards	1⅝ yards
Green	4 yards	5⅞ yards
Backing	7⅜ yards	8¼ yards
Batting	85" × 85"	94" × 114"
Binding	⅝ yard	1 yard

NOTE: *Yardages are based on 44/45-inch-wide fabrics that are at least 42 inches wide after preshrinking.*

CUTTING

All measurements include ¼-inch seam allowances. Referring to the Cutting Chart, cut the required number of strips in the width needed. Cut all strips across the fabric width (crosswise grain).

Cutting Chart

Fabric	Used For	Strip Width	Number to Cut Twin	Number to Cut Queen
Red	Baskets	2$\frac{3}{8}$"	8	13
	Baskets	24"	1	
	Baskets	35"		1
	Sashing strips	2$\frac{1}{2}$"	28	42
Orange	Baskets	24"	1	
	Baskets	35"		1
	Sashing squares	2$\frac{1}{2}$"	3	5
	Sashing triangles*	4$\frac{1}{4}$"	1	1
	Corner triangles*	1$\frac{7}{8}$"	1	1
Green	Basket background	9$\frac{7}{8}$"	6	9
	Basket sides	6$\frac{7}{8}$"	5	7
	Bottom triangles	3$\frac{7}{8}$"	3	4
	Setting triangles	14"	2	3

These pieces can be cut from scraps of other strips.

The basket block pieces are cut from strips. When you have cut the number of strips listed in the Cutting Chart, refer to the instructions here to cut the individual pieces. Many of the squares you cut will in turn be cut diagonally into halves or quarters, as shown in **Diagram 1**.

• For the red triangles for the baskets, cut the 2$\frac{3}{8}$-inch-wide strips into 2$\frac{3}{8}$-inch squares. Cut 135 squares for the twin size and 213 for the queen size, then cut the squares in half diagonally. You need six triangles per basket block.

• To cut the handles, refer to page 110 in "Basket Basics" on cutting bias strips. Each basket needs a 1 × 9$\frac{1}{2}$-inch bias strip that finishes to $\frac{3}{4}$ inch.

• For the red sashing strips, cut the 2$\frac{1}{2}$-inch-wide strips into 9-inch-long pieces. Cut 110 pieces for the twin-size quilt and 168 for the queen-size quilt.

• For the orange sashing squares, cut the 2$\frac{1}{2}$-inch-wide strips into 2$\frac{1}{2}$-inch squares. Cut 45 squares for the twin-size quilt and 72 squares for the queen-size quilt.

• For the orange sashing triangles, cut the 4$\frac{1}{4}$-inch-wide strip into 4$\frac{1}{4}$-inch squares. Cut five squares for the twin-size quilt and six squares for the queen-size quilt; cut each square diagonally both ways into four triangles.

• For the orange corner triangles for either size quilt, cut two 1$\frac{7}{8}$-inch squares, then cut the squares in half diagonally. These pieces can be cut from scraps.

• For the basket background triangles, cut the 9$\frac{7}{8}$-inch-wide green strips into twenty-three 9$\frac{7}{8}$-inch squares for the twin-size quilt and 36 squares for the queen size. Cut the squares in half diagonally.

• For the basket sides, cut the 6$\frac{7}{8}$-inch green strips into 2 × 6$\frac{7}{8}$-inch rectangles. Cut two rectangles for each block.

• For the bottom triangles of the basket blocks, cut the 3$\frac{7}{8}$-inch-wide green strips into 3$\frac{7}{8}$-inch squares. Cut each square in half diagonally to make two triangles.

• For the setting triangles, cut the 14-inch-wide green strips into 14-inch squares. Cut six squares for the twin-size quilt and seven squares for the queen-size quilt. Cut each square diagonally both ways into four triangles.

Note: Cut and piece one sample block before cutting all the fabric for the quilt.

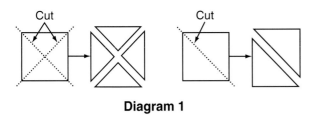

Diagram 1

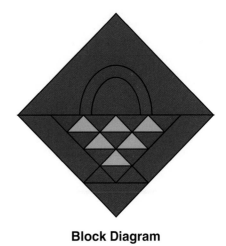

Block Diagram

Sew Quick

If you are making your quilt in the red, green, and orange color scheme, you may want to try this quick way to check your fabric for colorfastness, especially since red dyes are apt to run. After prewashing your fabric with vinegar or salt added to the water, snip a small swatch and pin it to a patch of white fabric. Swoosh the fabrics together in a basin of water. If the red dye runs onto the white fabric, you'll need to prewash the fabric again. If the fabric remains white, you're ready to start cutting.

PIECING THE BASKET BOTTOMS

Step 1. You will need red and orange triangle squares to complete each basket, as shown in the **Block Diagram.** The grid technique explained on page 106 in "Basket Basics" will help you to construct triangle squares more accurately and quickly than you could sewing single pairs of triangles together traditionally. Following the instructions on that page, use the 24- or 35-inch strips of red and orange fabric and a $2\frac{3}{8}$-inch grid to make the number of red and orange triangle squares required for your quilt.

Step 2. Position six red-and-orange triangle squares with four $2\frac{3}{8}$-inch red triangles, as shown in **Diagram 2.** Sew the pieces together in rows, as indicated. Press seams in opposite directions from one row to another. Stitch the four rows together, carefully matching seams as you work. Press.

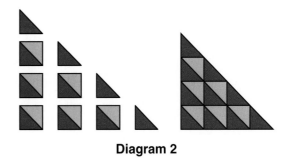

Diagram 2

Step 3. Stack two $2 \times 6\frac{7}{8}$-inch green rectangles together, matching edges carefully. Align the 45 degree line on your plastic ruler with the edge of the rectangles, as shown in **Diagram 3.** Cut diago-

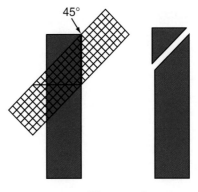

Diagram 3

nally, making sure the angled cut is positioned to begin at the corner of the rectangle, as shown. The green triangles you cut away from each rectangle won't be used in the basket, but they may come in handy for another project.

Note: If you are using a one-sided background fabric, the rectangles must be cut as mirror images. Stack each pair with wrong sides together, then trim.

Step 4. Sew a 2³⁄₈-inch red triangle to the straight end of the two green pieces you just cut, as shown in **Diagram 4**.

Diagram 4

Step 5. Sew the units to either side of the partially assembled basket, as shown in **Diagram 5**. Align the pieces where seams meet, pressing seams in opposite directions before sewing.

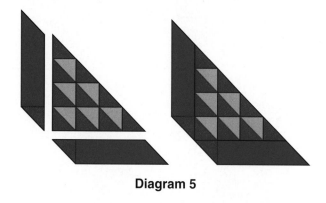

Diagram 5

Step 6. Sew a 3⁷⁄₈-inch green triangle to the bottom of the basket, as shown in **Diagram 6**, completing the bottom half of the basket.

Step 7. Repeat Steps 2 through 6 to make 40 basket bottoms for the twin-size quilt and 71 basket bottoms for the queen-size quilt.

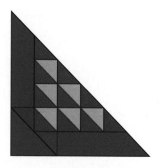

Diagram 6

APPLIQUÉING THE BASKET HANDLES

We recommend that you use bias strips for the handles of your baskets, since they can easily be shaped into curves. You will find complete instructions for that method and other tips for constructing handles on page 110 in "Basket Basics." The finished width of your handles should be approximately ³⁄₄ inch. Each handle should be approximately 9¹⁄₂ inches long. Although a matching thread and straight machine stitch were used to sew the handles onto the quilt shown, any hand-appliqué technique you prefer will work equally as well.

Step 1. Prepare the handles for the appliqué method of your choice.

Step 2. Appliqué a handle to a 9⁷⁄₈-inch green triangle. The outside edges of the handle should be approximately 4 inches from the right and left edges of the triangle. The top curve of the handle should be approximately 3¹⁄₄ inches from the top point of the triangle, as shown in **Diagram 7**.

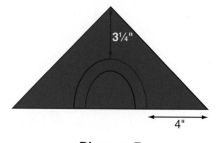

Diagram 7

Sew Easy

To get the shape for your handles just right, use a quilter's flexible curve. This handy tool, available at most quilt shops, is great for designing curved pieces such as stems, leaves, and other appliqué shapes. For this project, bend the flexible curve to a handle shape that's pleasing to you. Place the curve on your background fabric and lightly trace its outline. Appliqué your handle over the traced lines. Use the same curve shape for each basket for a perfectly matched set of handles.

Step 3. After the handle has been appliquéd to the large triangle, sew the two block halves together. See the **Block Diagram** on page 19.

Step 4. Repeat Steps 1 through 3 to complete the required number of basket blocks for your quilt.

ASSEMBLING THE QUILT TOP

Step 1. Use a design wall or other flat surface to lay out your basket blocks, setting triangles, and sashing strips, squares, and triangles, referring to the **Assembly Diagram.**

Step 2. Sew all pieces into diagonal rows, as shown. Press the seams toward the red sashing strips. Sew the rows together, matching seams carefully. Sew the four corner triangles on last. Press the quilt.

QUILTING AND FINISHING

Step 1. Mark the quilt top for quilting, if desired. The twin-size quilt shown in the **Quilt Diagram** on page 22 was quilted in an allover diagonal crosshatch pattern, using the triangles of the baskets as a guide.

Step 2. Regardless of which quilt size you've chosen to make, the backing will have to be

Assembly Diagram

pieced. **Diagram 8** illustrates the two quilt backs. To make the backing for the twin-size quilt, divide the backing fabric crosswise into three equal pieces, and trim the selvages.

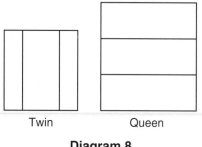

Twin   Queen

Diagram 8

Step 3. Cut a 24-inch lengthwise piece from two of the pieces. Sew a 24-inch piece to each side of the full-width piece. Press the seams open.

Step 4. To make the backing for the queen-size quilt, divide the fabric crosswise into three equal

pieces, and trim the selvages. Sew the three pieces together along the long edges, and press the seams open.

Step 5. Layer the quilt top, batting, and backing, and baste the layers together. Quilt as desired.

Step 6. You'll notice that no binding is evident in the original quilt. The binding was sewn to the quilt, then pressed and turned completely to the back and stitched in place by hand. The original quilt contains a very thin cotton batting, so the seam turned easily. If you prefer to make a conventional double-fold binding, refer to page 121 in "Quiltmaking Basics" for directions. To calculate the amount of binding needed for the quilt size you are making, add up the length of the four sides of the quilt and add 9 inches. The total is the approximate number of inches of binding you will need.

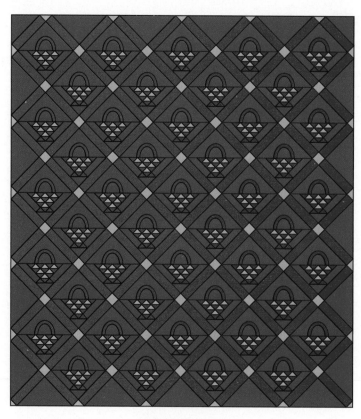

Quilt Diagram

RED-AND-ORANGE BASKETS
Color Plan

Photocopy this page and use it to experiment with color schemes for your quilt.

BLUEBIRDS OF HAPPINESS

Skill Level: *Intermediate*

*T*his charming twin-size appliqué quilt was made in Bucks County, Pennsylvania, in the early- or mid-1930s by the grandmother or great-aunt of its current owner. Bluebirds of Happiness is an adaptation of Garden Bouquet, a block-a-week pattern that ran in a nationally syndicated newspaper column called the "Nancy Page Quilt Club" in 1932.

BEFORE YOU BEGIN

The background pieces and borders for this quilt are rotary cut from strips. For each of the appliqué shapes, you will need to make a template from the patterns on pages 32–33. Refer to page 116 in "Quiltmaking Basics" for instructions on making and using templates.

The quilt shown has a different flower in each appliqué block. Patterns are provided for four flowers, a basket, birds, and wings. Make several of each flower pattern provided or make a larger variety of flowers for your quilt.

CHOOSING FABRICS

The quiltmaker chose a variety of flowers found in spring and summer gardens to fill the baskets of her quilt. The baskets themselves and the pair of bluebirds perched on each one remain the same from block to block. You can use colorful calico scraps to make the flowers, or you may want to purchase reproduction fabrics of the 1930s era. Many delightful prints are available today in bright colors such as bubblegum pink, yellow, lavender, orange, blue, and green. To develop your own color scheme, photocopy the **Color Plan** on page 31, and use crayons or colored pencils to plan your color choices.

Quilt Sizes

	Twin (shown)	Queen
Finished Quilt Size	70" × 85"	85" × 99³⁄₄"
Finished Block Size	10¹⁄₂"	10¹⁄₂"
Number of Basket Blocks	20	30
Number of Setting Squares	12	20

Materials

	Twin	Queen
Muslin	3 yards	4 yards
Blue solid	3¹⁄₂ yards	5 yards
Tan	⁵⁄₈ yard	1 yard
Blue print	¹⁄₃ yard	¹⁄₂ yard
Green	³⁄₈ yard	⁵⁄₈ yard
Assorted prints	Scraps	Scraps
Gold	¹⁄₈ yard or scraps	¹⁄₈ yard or scraps
Backing	5¹⁄₄ yards	7⁷⁄₈ yards
Batting	76" × 91"	91" × 106"
Binding	⁵⁄₈ yard	³⁄₄ yard
Gold embroidery floss	1 skein	1 skein
Black embroidery floss	1 skein	1 skein

NOTE: Yardages are based on 44/45-inch-wide fabrics that are at least 42 inches wide after preshrinking.

Cutting Chart

Fabric	Used For	Strip Width	Number of Strips	
			Twin	Queen
Muslin	Background squares	11"	7	10
	Inner border	2½"	9	11
Blue solid	Setting squares	11"	4	7
	Side setting triangles and corner setting triangles	16⅛"	2	3
	Outer border	3½"	9	12
	Bird 1		20	30
	Bird 2 wing		20	30
Tan	Baskets		20	30
Blue print	Bird 2		20	30
	Bird 1 wing		20	30
Green	Leaves*			
Assorted prints	Flowers*			

See specific cutting information for leaves and flowers in the text. Cutting these pieces may vary depending on the type of flowers and leaves you choose.

CUTTING

The measurements for the background blocks, setting squares, side setting triangles, and borders include ¼-inch seam allowances. Referring to the Cutting Chart, cut the required strips across the fabric width. For the background and setting squares, cut the 11-inch-wide strips into 11-inch squares. For the side setting triangles, cut the 16⅛-inch strips into 16⅛-inch squares. Cut the squares diagonally both ways. (See **Diagram 1**.) For the corner setting triangles, cut two 8⅜-inch squares from the leftover 16⅛-inch-wide strips. Cut the squares in half diagonally one way.

For the appliqué pieces, make templates using the full-size patterns on pages 32–33, then cut the number of pieces required. Add seam allowances when cutting them from fabric. For the stems, cut ¾-inch-wide bias strips that finish ½ inch wide. You need about 3½ inches in length for each block.

Note: Cut and stitch one sample block before cutting all the fabric for the quilt.

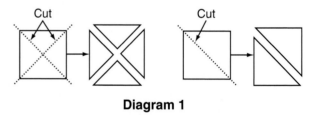

Diagram 1

PREPARING THE APPLIQUÉ PIECES

Each appliqué block has one basket, two birds, and one floral centerpiece. The basket and birds are the same for each block. The flowers vary from block to block. Follow the directions below to make one lily block. After completing the block, repeat the steps to make the remainder of the blocks needed for your quilt.

Step 1. One-half of the basket pattern is given. Trace it twice onto tracing paper, then flip one half-basket over to create a mirror image, butting its edges with the other half. Use the image to make a whole basket template. Carefully cut out the holes in the handles.

Step 2. To prepare the basket for appliqué, we recommend that you use either of the freezer paper techniques explained on page 108 in "Basket Basics." Turn under edges carefully, clipping into sharp inner points.

Step 3. Bird 1 (on the left of the flower) is made from a blue solid body, blue print wing, and gold beak. Prepare one of each for appliqué. The inner portion of the beak is left unfinished as indicated by the dotted line on the pattern. Set pieces aside while you finish other block elements.

Step 4. Bird 2 (on the right of the flower) is made from a blue print body, a blue solid wing, and a gold beak. Prepare one of each for appliqué in the same manner as you did for Bird 1.

Step 5. The flower stems are made from green bias strips with a finished width of $^1/_2$ inch. See page 110 in "Basket Basics" for complete information on constructing bias strips.

Step 6. Prepare the flower and leaves for the lily from the templates you made earlier. The pattern on page 33 indicates color placement.

APPLIQUÉING THE LILY BLOCK

Step 1. Fold an 11-inch muslin background square diagonally and finger press it. Fold on the other diagonal and finger press. Fold horizontally, then vertically, finger pressing after each fold. The resulting creases will help you position the appliqué pieces symmetrically.

Step 2. Refer to the **Lily Block Diagram** to position the pieces for the block. Center the basket along the vertical crease with its base approximately $2^3/_4$ inches from the bottom point of the square. Pin in place.

Step 3. Cut a $3^1/_2$-inch-long piece from a green bias strip. Tuck one end under the top edge of the basket, then curve the stem slightly as you pin it to the muslin square, referring to the block dia-

Lily Block Diagram

gram for placement. Tuck the tip of each leaf under the stem. Pin the pieces in place. Position the lily blossom and petals so they overlap the stem end by approximately $^1/_4$ inch.

Step 4. Position the body of Bird 1 slightly above the basket on the left side of the leaves, with its head looking upward. Position the wing on top of the body, as shown, and tuck the unfinished edge of the beak under the head. Pin the pieces in place.

Step 5. In a similar manner, position Bird 2 above the basket on the right side, but with its head tilted slightly downward. Pin in place.

Step 6. Examine the block to be sure you like the layout. Reposition any pieces as desired. Make sure the design elements do not fall within the $^1/_4$-inch seam allowance around the block. When you are satisfied with the layout, baste the pieces to the square and remove the pins.

Step 7. The legs of each bird are hand embroidered to the block using gold floss and a chain stitch. Embroider the legs now, before appliquéing the birds to the block, so you can easily end each line of stitching underneath the body of the birds. Refer to page 111 in "Basket Basics" for more information on embroidery stitches.

Step 8. Appliqué each piece to the block using matching thread and a blind stitch. Use black floss to make a French knot for the eye of each bird as well as for the stamens of the lily.

Step 9. Repeat Steps 1 through 8 to make the number of blocks required for your quilt. Instructions for three more flowers are given below. Prepare the baskets and birds for each block as stated previously. Only the floral portions differ. Use the first block as a guide when positioning baskets and birds on remaining squares.

APPLIQUÉING THE PANSY, STAR FLOWER, AND DAFFODIL BLOCKS

Step 1. Prepare the pieces for each of these flowers from the templates you made earlier. The patterns on page 33 give color recommendations, but you may use any colors you like for the blossoms. The dotted lines on the patterns indicate where pieces overlap.

Step 2. Cut a 3-inch stem from the green bias strip for each block, then position it as you did with the lily block, tucking one raw edge of the stem under the basket. Curve the stems slightly and pin them to the muslin squares. Pin leaves along the stem, positioning their tips behind the stem.

Step 3. Refer to the block diagrams for the layout of each flower. Position the pieces on the squares, as shown, overlapping them as indicated on the patterns. Baste the pieces to each square when you are satisfied with the appearance.

Step 4. Appliqué all of the pieces to the block using matching thread and a blind stitch. Embroider the birds' legs and eyes and the flower centers.

COMPLETING THE BLOCKS

We have given patterns for making four different blocks. Repeat these four blocks throughout your quilt or use other floral centerpieces for your baskets. The quilt pictured has many flowers, ranging from daffodils to daisies to a cactus in bloom! Use your imagination and colorful scraps to make this quilt truly your own.

Pansy Block Diagram

Star Flower Block Diagram

Daffodil Block Diagram

ASSEMBLING THE QUILT TOP

Step 1. Lay out the appliqué blocks, setting squares, side setting triangles, and corner setting triangles in diagonal rows. The **Assembly Diagram** shows the layout for the twin-size quilt. For the queen-size quilt, you will have six rows of baskets with five basket blocks in each row. Move the appliqué blocks around until the arrangement pleases you, then sew the blocks together into diagonal rows. Press the seams toward the blue setting squares and triangles.

Step 2. Sew the rows together, matching seams carefully. Press the quilt top.

ADDING THE MITERED BORDERS

This quilt has a 2-inch inner muslin border and a 3-inch outer blue solid border. Sew the muslin and blue strips together first, then add them to the quilt top as a single unit, mitering the corners.

Assembly Diagram

Step 1. To determine the correct length for the side borders, measure the quilt top vertically through the center. To this measurement, add two times the finished width of the border (5 inches × 2 = 10 inches), plus 5 inches. This is the length you will need to make the two side borders. In the same manner, measure the quilt top horizontally through the center to calculate the length of the top and bottom borders.

Step 2. Before you can sew the muslin and blue border strips together, you will need to sew the muslin border strips together end to end until you've achieved the required lengths for each border. Repeat for the blue border strips. **Diagram 2** illustrates the placement of border strips.

Diagram 2

Step 3. Working with the side border strips first, pin and sew the blue and muslin strips together lengthwise into two units. Press seams toward the blue border. In the same manner, pin and sew the top and bottom border strips together into two units. Press seams toward the muslin.

Step 4. Pin and sew the four border units to the quilt top. Refer to page 119 in "Quiltmaking Basics" for instructions on adding borders with mitered corners. When preparing the miters, be sure to match like strips in adjacent borders, as shown in the **Quilt Diagram** on page 30.

QUILTING AND FINISHING

Step 1. Mark the top for quilting. The quilt shown was outline quilted around the appliqués. A tulip design was quilted in the blue squares.

Step 2. Regardless of which quilt size you've chosen to make, the backing will have to be pieced. **Diagram 3** illustrates the layout for both quilt backs. For the twin-size quilt, divide the backing fabric crosswise into two equal pieces, and trim the selvages. Cut one segment in half lengthwise, then sew a narrow segment to each side of the full-width piece. Press the seams open.

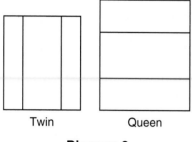

Twin   Queen

Diagram 3

Step 3. For the queen-size quilt, divide the backing fabric crosswise into three equal pieces, and trim the selvages. Measure and cut a 34-inch-wide piece from two of the segments, and sew one piece to each side of the full-width segment, as shown in the diagram. Press the seams open.

Step 4. Layer the quilt top, batting, and backing, and baste the layers together. Quilt all marked designs and add other quilting as desired.

Step 5. Referring to the directions on page 121 in "Quiltmaking Basics," make and attach double-fold binding. Add the length of the four sides of the quilt plus 9 inches to calculate the number of inches of binding you will need.

Quilt Diagram

BLUEBIRDS OF HAPPINESS
Color Plan

Photocopy this page and use it to experiment with color schemes for your quilt.

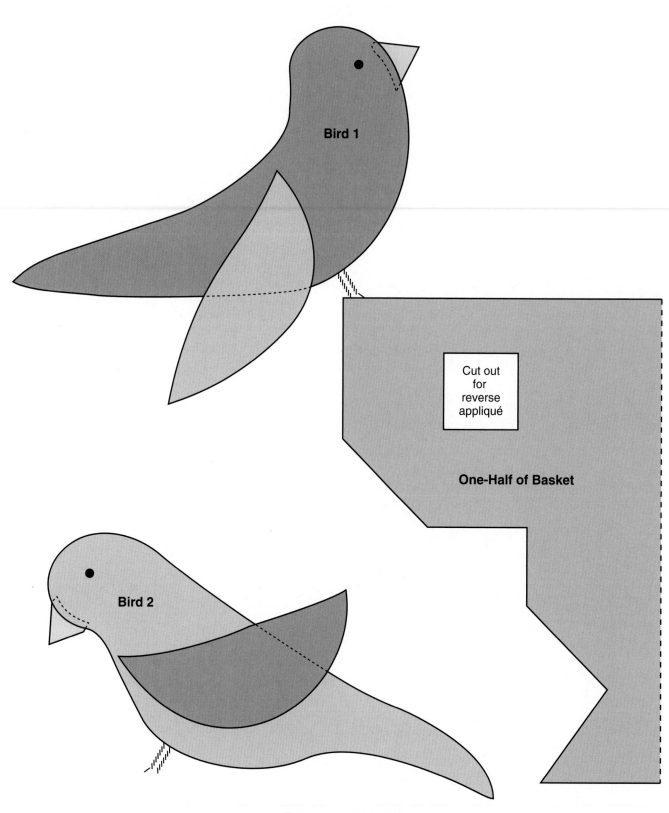

Bird 1

Cut out
for
reverse
appliqué

One-Half of Basket

Bird 2

Patterns are finished size.
Add seam allowances when cutting.

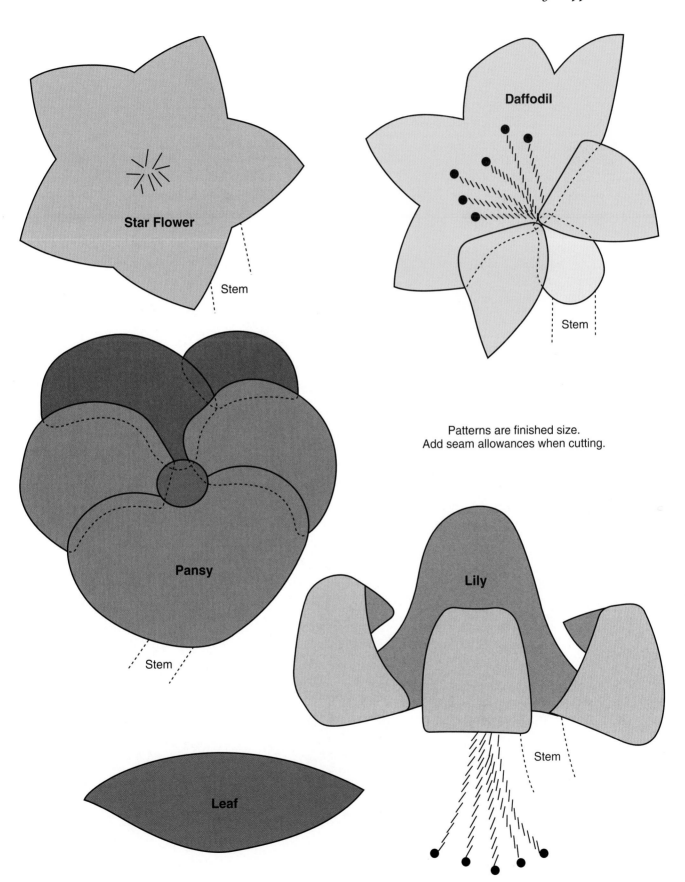

Star Flower

Stem

Daffodil

Stem

Patterns are finished size.
Add seam allowances when cutting.

Pansy

Stem

Lily

Stem

Leaf

Amish Easter Baskets

Skill Level: *Intermediate*

he rich dark colors of the Cake Stand Baskets stitched together in an unusual Bear's Paw-type setting make a dramatic statement in this queen-size quilt. The quilt design was patterned after a similar but smaller antique quilt. In addition to expert piecing and quilting, this quilt also shows off the maker's appliqué talents with the final touch of a hand-appliquéd sawtooth edging on the outer border. The quiltmaker was inspired to add "Amish" to the name of this quilt because of all the dark solids she used.

BEFORE YOU BEGIN

The directions for this quilt are written for rotary cutting and quick piecing. Yardage requirements include enough fabric to cut borders lengthwise before other pieces are cut from the fabric. This method takes advantage of the stability that the lengthwise grain adds to the borders. It also avoids seams in the borders, which are more likely to show on solid fabrics than on prints.

CHOOSING FABRICS

This quilt is made entirely of solid fabrics, including unbleached muslin. When selecting the dark solids, choose high-quality fabrics. These have a tight weave or high thread count and do not feel as though the dyes will rub off between your fingers. For an authentic Amish feel, consider using black in place of the muslin and traditional Amish brights in place of the navy, red, and green.

To help develop your own unique color scheme for the quilt, photocopy the **Color Plan** on page 41, and use crayons or colored pencils to experiment with different color arrangements.

Quilt Sizes		
	Lap	**Queen (shown)**
Finished Quilt Size	60½" × 87"	87" × 113½"
Finished Block Size		
Single Basket	7½"	7½"
Four Basket	19"	19"
Number of Blocks		
Single Basket	24	48
Four Basket	6	12

Materials		
	Lap	**Queen**
Unbleached muslin	4 yards	5¾ yards
Navy blue	2½ yards	3¼ yards
Dark red	2½ yards	3¼ yards
Dark green	1 yard	1⅜ yards
Backing	5⅛ yards	7⅔ yards
Batting	67" × 93"	93" × 120"

NOTE: *Yardages are based on 44/45-inch-wide fabrics that are at least 42 inches wide after preshrinking.*

CUTTING

All measurements include ¼-inch seam allowances. Cut all borders, binding, and piping

Cutting Chart

Fabric	Used For	Lengthwise Strip Width	Number to Cut Lap	Queen
Muslin	Border	8"	4	4
Navy	Piping	3/4"	4	4
Red	Sawtooth border	2"	4	4
	Binding	1½"	4	4

Fabric	Used For	Crosswise Strip Width	Number to Cut* Lap	Queen
Muslin	Sashing strips	8"	4	9
	Block background	2"	8	14
	Basket handles	2³⁄₈"	5	9
	Bottom triangles	3⁷⁄₈"	2	3
Navy	Sashing/border squares	8"	2	3
	Sashing strips	8"	3	6
Red	Baskets	5³⁄₈"	4	7
	Basket handles	2³⁄₈"	7	14
	Center squares	4½"	1	2
Green	Basket bottoms	5³⁄₈"	4	7
	Basket feet	2³⁄₈"	2	3

Calculations are based on the fabric widths remaining after cutting the lengthwise pieces. Muslin strips are based on 42-inch-wide strips.

first, cutting on the lengthwise grain to minimize seams. Cut a 100-inch-long piece from the muslin for the queen-size quilt and a 75-inch-long piece for the lap-size quilt; you'll cut border strips from these lengths. Next, referring to the Cutting Chart, cut the required number of lengthwise strips in the width needed from the previously cut muslin lengths as well as from the navy and red fabrics. After you have finished the lengthwise cutting, refer to the second part of the Cutting Chart and cut the crosswise strips. When you have cut all of those strips, refer to the instructions that follow to cut the *crosswise* strips into individual pieces.

• For the sashing strips, cut the 8-inch-wide muslin strips into 19½-inch-long pieces. Cut 17 for the queen-size quilt and 7 for the lap size.

• For the block background, cut the 2-inch-wide muslin strips into 2 × 5-inch rectangles. Cut 96 rectangles for the queen-size quilt and 48 for the lap size. From the remaining strips, cut 2-inch squares: 48 for the queen size and 24 for the lap size.

• For the bottom triangles of the basket blocks, cut the 3⁷⁄₈-inch-wide muslin strips into 3⁷⁄₈-inch squares. Cut the squares in half diagonally, as shown in **Diagram 1**. Make 48 triangles for the queen-size quilt and 24 for the lap size.

• For the basket handles, cut the 2³⁄₈-inch-wide muslin strips into 2³⁄₈-inch squares. Cut the squares in half diagonally to make 288 triangles for the queen size and 144 triangles for the lap size.

• For the sashing and border squares, cut the 8-inch-wide navy strips into 8-inch squares. Cut ten for the queen size and six for the lap size.

• For the sashing strips in the basket blocks, cut the 8-inch-wide navy strips into 4½ × 8-inch rectangles. You need 48 for the queen size and 24 for the lap size.

• For the top half of the baskets, cut the 5⅜-inch-wide red strips into 5⅜-inch squares. Cut the squares in half diagonally.

• For the basket handles, cut the 2⅜-inch-wide red strips into 2⅜-inch squares. Cut the squares in half diagonally to make 288 triangles for the queen-size quilt and 144 for the lap size.

• For the center squares of the four-basket blocks, cut the 4½-inch-wide red strips into 4½-inch squares. You need 12 squares for the queen-size quilt and 6 for the lap size.

• For the basket bottoms, cut the 5⅜-inch-wide green strips into 5⅜-inch squares. Cut the squares in half diagonally, as shown.

• For the basket feet, cut the 2⅜-inch-wide green strips into 2⅜-inch squares. Cut the squares in half diagonally, as shown.

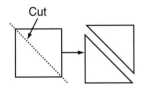

Diagram 1

PIECING THE BASKET BLOCKS

Step 1. Sew 5⅜-inch red and green triangles together to form a triangle square for the center of the basket block, as shown in **Diagram 2.**

Diagram 2

Step 2. Sew the 2⅜-inch muslin and red triangles together to form triangle squares. You will need six red-and-muslin triangle squares per basket. Press the seams toward the red fabric.

Step 3. Sew the triangle squares together in strips of three, referring to **Diagram 3** for color placement. Add a muslin square to the end of one strip, as shown in the diagram.

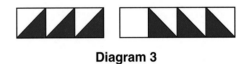

Diagram 3

Step 4. Attach the shorter triangle-square strip to the large red-and-green triangle square, as shown in **Diagram 4.** Sew the other triangle-square strip to the block, as shown.

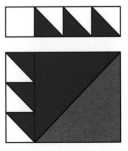

Diagram 4

Step 5. Sew a 2⅜-inch green triangle to the end of a muslin rectangle. Make two such units for each basket, referring to **Diagram 5** for placement of the triangles.

Diagram 5

Step 6. Sew the rectangle units to the green sides of the partial block. Press the seams toward the rectangles. To complete the single-basket block, add a muslin triangle to the corner, as shown in the **Block Diagram.** Press the seam away from the muslin.

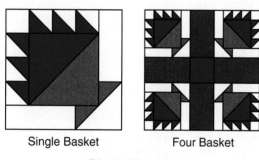

Single Basket   Four Basket

Block Diagram

Step 7. Repeat Steps 1 through 6 to make 48 basket blocks for the queen-size quilt and 24 blocks for the lap-size quilt.

ASSEMBLING THE QUILT TOP

The individual basket blocks are assembled into larger blocks containing four basket blocks separated by navy sashing strips, as shown in the **Block Diagram.** The four-basket blocks are then pieced together with muslin sashing strips and navy sashing squares.

Step 1. To make a four-basket block, lay out four baskets, four navy sashing strips, and one red center square in three horizontal rows. Make sure each basket handle points toward a corner.

Step 2. Stitch the units together into rows. Press the seams toward the navy sashing strips. Sew the rows together. Press the seams toward the navy strips. The finished block should measure 19½ inches square, including seam allowances. Repeat to make 12 four-basket blocks for the queen-size quilt and 6 blocks for the lap quilt.

Step 3. Referring to the **Assembly Diagram,** lay out the blocks, muslin sashing strips, and navy sashing squares in rows. The quilt shown is the queen size. For the lap size, you'll have only three horizontal rows of two blocks each, with two muslin/navy sashing strip units between them.

Step 4. Sew the blocks and sashing pieces together into rows. Press the seams toward the sashing. Sew the rows together, matching seam intersections. Press all seams in one direction.

ADDING THE BORDERS

The muslin borders and navy corner squares are stitched to the quilt, then a red sawtooth

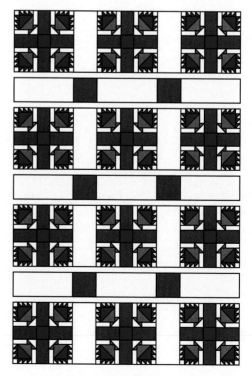

Assembly Diagram

border is appliquéd to the edge. The navy piping is added during the binding stage.

Step 1. Measure the width of the quilt top through the center of the quilt rather than along the top or bottom edge. Cut two border strips to this exact length. Measure the length of the quilt top, again through the center of the quilt. Cut the remaining strips to this exact length.

Step 2. Fold one short border strip in half crosswise and crease. Unfold it and position it right side down along the top edge of the quilt, with the crease at the midpoint. Pin at the midpoint and ends first, then along the length of the entire end, easing in fullness if necessary. Sew the border to the quilt top using a ¼-inch seam allowance. Press the seam toward the border. Repeat to add the border to the bottom of the quilt.

Step 3. Sew a navy border corner square to each end of the two side borders. Stitch the borders to the quilt sides as you did for the top and bottom borders, matching seam lines, pinning at the midpoints, and easing in fullness if necessary.

Step 4. To make the sawtooth border, make a mark every 2 inches along the length of one side of the 2-inch-wide red strip, beginning at one end, as shown in **Diagram 6**. On the opposite side of the strip, make a mark 1 inch from the end. Continue making marks every 2 inches so they are halfway between those on the other side. Mark the remaining strips in this manner.

Diagram 6

Step 5. Pin a red strip to the outside edge of the quilt border, and baste it in place with a ¼-inch seam allowance. On the unbasted edge of the strip, cut diagonally from one mark to the next mark on the opposite edge. Cut up to the ¼-inch seam, as shown in **Diagram 7**. Use the line of basting as a handy guide to know when to stop cutting.

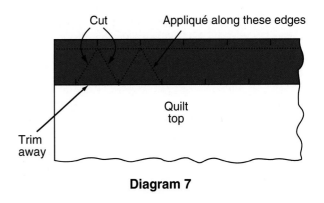

Diagram 7

Step 6. Turn under the fabric in a diagonal line from one mark to the opposite mark to make a sawtooth point. Trim away excess fabric if necessary. Appliqué the point in place, using the needle-turn appliqué method described on page 118 in "Quiltmaking Basics." Repeat for all borders.

Sew Easy

You will find it much easier to appliqué your sawtooth border if you snip only one or two sawtooth points at a time. You will reduce the chance of stretching your border fabric out of shape and increase the chance of a flat, nicely fitted border.

QUILTING AND FINISHING

Step 1. Mark the top for quilting. The quilt shown was quilted with a double pumpkin seed pattern in the red squares, a feathered square in the navy sashing squares, and a serpentine feather in the sashing strips. Diagonal lines about ¼ inch apart fill in the background of the muslin. Each basket was quilted in diagonal lines from the top corner above the basket point to the corner below the base. The lines continue through the navy sashing squares, where they form a crosshatch design.

Step 2. Regardless of which quilt size you've chosen to make, the backing will have to be pieced. For the lap quilt, divide the 5⅛ yards of backing fabric into two equal length pieces, and trim the selvages. Cut one of the pieces in half lengthwise, and sew one half to each side of the full piece (see **Diagram 8**). Press the seams open.

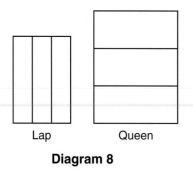

Lap   Queen

Diagram 8

Step 3. For the queen-size quilt, divide the 7²/₃ yards of fabric crosswise into three equal pieces, and trim the selvages. Sew the three pieces together along the long sides, as shown in **Diagram 8,** and press the seams open.

Step 4. Layer the quilt top, batting, and backing; baste the layers together. Quilt as desired.

Step 5. To add the navy piping, fold the ³/₄-inch strips in half lengthwise, right sides together, and press. Lay one strip along one edge of the quilt top, with raw edges even. Hand baste in place. Add a piping strip to each side of the quilt in the same manner, making sure the strip extends to the edge of the quilt on each end. Then, referring to the directions on page 121 in "Quilt-making Basics," make and attach double-fold binding. Add the lengths of the four sides of the quilt plus 9 inches to calculate the number of inches of binding you will need. After the binding is attached, about ¹/₈ inch of navy piping will be visible, as evident in the **Quilt Diagram.**

Quilt Diagram

AMISH EASTER BASKETS
Color Plan

Photocopy this page and use it to experiment with color schemes for your quilt.

41

Carolina Lily Medallion

Skill Level: *Challenging*

B y the time this quilt was pieced in the 1920s or perhaps the 1930s, the North Carolina Lily block was already quite popular. While the block design itself was not original, the maker of this twin-size quilt certainly showed her creativity by her innovative placement of the blocks, resulting in a unique medallion-style quilt. This quilt is from Seminole, Oklahoma, where it was apparently used as a bed-spread, perhaps in a guest room, since it shows little sign of the wear and tear of an everyday quilt.

BEFORE YOU BEGIN

This quilt is made of eight pieced blocks set in a medallion-style arrangement. Each block requires setting in several pieces, so it might be helpful to read through the instructions on page 117 in "Quiltmaking Basics" first to make sure you understand this technique. Because there are many pieces in each block, accurate cutting and stitching are a must for this project. While we don't recommend tackling this project if you are a beginner, you'll have no problem creating your own heirloom Carolina Lily Medallion quilt if you have mastered rotary-cutting skills and enjoy the challenge of working with set-in pieces.

CHOOSING FABRICS

Each flower blossom has two light and two dark petals. All fabrics are solids, and they are set together in coordinating shades. For example, the quilt shown uses a variety of colors in its flowers, but each individual flower uses a dark and a light of the same color, such as light and dark blue, lavender and purple, or light peach and orange. You should be able to cut eight flower petals from each 10 × 10-inch piece of fabric, which means a dozen pieces would be enough to complete the quilt. However, be sure to choose six pairs of fabrics that coordinate. Or, if you'd like to have a wider variety of flowers in your quilt, simply choose more fabrics.

To help develop your own unique color scheme for the

Quilt Size	
Finished Quilt Size	74½" × 84½"
Finished Block Size	14"
Number of Blocks	8

NOTE: Due to the complexity of the design, no size variations are provided.

Materials	
Fabric	**Amount**
Muslin	5¼ yards
Green	¾ yard
Brown	⅓ yard
Assorted solids	approx. 10" × 10" square of 12 colors
Backing	5¼ yards
Batting	80" × 90"
Binding	⅝ yard

NOTE: Yardages are based on 44/45-inch-wide fabrics that are at least 42 inches wide after preshrinking.

Step 4. Sew a muslin C square to the blossom unit, as shown in **Diagram 5,** setting in the seam where indicated by the black dot. Press the seams toward the muslin square.

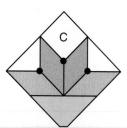

Diagram 5

Step 5. Sew a muslin E triangle to each side of the blossom unit, as shown in **Diagram 6.** Press the seams toward the muslin. Set the unit aside for now.

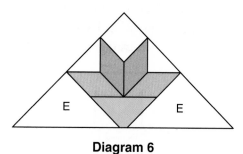

Diagram 6

Step 6. To complete the assembly of the remaining two blossoms, sew a green F triangle to the bottom of each unit, as shown in **Diagram 7.** Press the seams toward the green triangles.

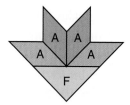

Diagram 7

Step 7. Sew two muslin C squares and one muslin D triangle to each unit, as shown in **Diagram 8,** setting in seams where indicated by the dots. Press the seams toward the muslin pieces. Set the units aside while you construct the stem unit.

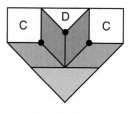

Diagram 8

Step 8. Referring to **Diagram 9,** place three bias stems on a muslin G rectangle. Position and pin the straight center stem first, then the two curving stems. Begin at the top of the rectangle and gently curve the stems toward the bottom. The stem ends should extend to the edges of the rectangle; cut away any excess. Appliqué the stems in place.

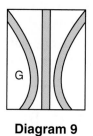

Diagram 9

Sew Easy

To avoid tangling your thread when you appliqué the stems to the block, try using sequin pins to hold your fabric in place. These short pins, available in craft and fabric stores, reduce the chance of catching your thread on pins. Another option is to pin your stems from the back of your block fabric. With the pin points underneath, you won't be apt to tangle your thread.

Step 9. Sew the Step 7 blossom units to the completed stem unit, as shown in **Diagram 10.** Press the seams toward the stem unit.

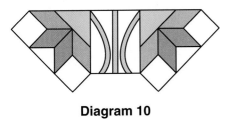

Diagram 10

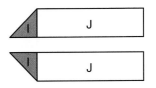

Diagram 13

Step 10. Sew the last blossom unit to the Step 9 unit, as shown in **Diagram 11.** Press the seams toward the blossom unit just added.

Step 13. Sew the I/J units from Step 12 to the partially assembled block, as shown in **Diagram 14.** Press the seams toward the I/J units.

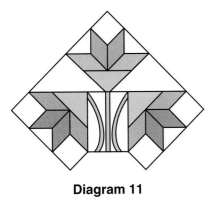

Diagram 11

Step 11. Sew a brown H piece to the bottom of the partially assembled block, as shown in **Diagram 12,** setting in the seams where indicated by the dots. Press the seams toward the brown piece.

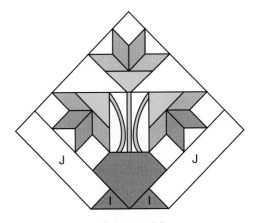

Diagram 14

Step 14. Sew a muslin K triangle to the bottom of the basket to complete the block. Press the seam toward the muslin triangle.

Step 15. Repeat Steps 1 through 14 to make a total of eight blocks.

ASSEMBLING THE QUILT TOP

Step 1. Sew two lily blocks to the ends of a muslin sashing strip, as shown in **Diagram 15.** Repeat, making two identical units.

Diagram 12

Step 12. Sew two brown I triangles to two muslin J rectangles, as shown in **Diagram 13.**

Diagram 15

Quilt Diagram

Step 2. Sew four lily blocks together, as shown in **Diagram 16**, then sew one of the remaining sashing strips to each side of the unit, as indicated. Press the seams toward the sashing strips.

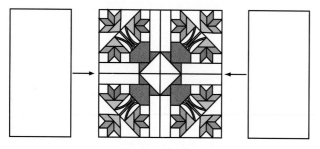

Diagram 16

Step 3. Sew the Step 1 units to the center unit, making sure the tops of the lilies point toward the center of the quilt. Use the photo on page 42 or the **Quilt Diagram** as a guide to placement. Press the seams toward the muslin sashing strips.

ADDING THE BORDERS

Step 1. The border strips must be pieced to achieve the required length. For the top and bottom borders, piece together three 14½-inch-wide strips. Cut the strip in half to make two long borders. Measure the width of the quilt, taking the measurement through the horizontal center rather than along the edge. Trim the border strips to this exact measured length.

Step 2. Fold one strip in half crosswise and crease. Unfold it and position it right side down along the top edge of the quilt, with the crease at the vertical midpoint. Pin at the midpoint and ends first, then along the width of the quilt, easing in fullness if necessary. Sew the border to the quilt using a ¼-inch seam allowance. Press the seam toward the border. Repeat on the opposite end.

Step 3. For the side borders, piece together the five 9½-inch-wide strips; cut the strip in half to make two long borders. Measure the length of the quilt, taking the measurement through the vertical center of the quilt and including the top and bottom borders. Trim the border strips to this exact measured length.

Step 4. In the same manner as for the top and bottom borders, position and pin a strip on one side of the quilt, easing in fullness if necessary. Stitch, using a ¼-inch seam allowance. Press the seam toward the border. Repeat on the opposite side.

QUILTING AND FINISHING

Step 1. Mark the quilt top for quilting. The antique quilt shown was quilted with a crosshatch design in the muslin areas. A smaller-scale crosshatching was used to quilt the brown baskets. Other shapes were outline quilted.

Step 2. To piece the quilt back, first cut the backing fabric crosswise into two equal pieces, and trim the selvages.

Step 3. Cut one of the segments in half lengthwise, and sew one half to each side of the full-width piece. Press the seams open.

Step 4. Layer the backing, batting, and quilt top; baste. Quilt as desired.

Step 5. Referring to the directions on page 121 in "Quiltmaking Basics," make and attach double-fold binding. To calculate the amount of binding needed for your quilt, add up the length of the four sides of the quilt and add 9 inches. The total is the approximate number of inches of binding you will need.

········· Sew Quick ·········

An easy way to mark crosshatch lines for quilting is to simply use masking tape. It comes in ¾- and 1-inch widths, so you can pick the width that suits you best. Keep the tape on the quilt only while stitching. Take it off when you set the quilt aside and *never* press over it. Look for fresh tape; older tape tends to have more of a gummy residue, which could be left on the quilt top.

CAROLINA LILY MEDALLION
Color Plan

Photocopy this page and use it to experiment with color schemes for your quilt.

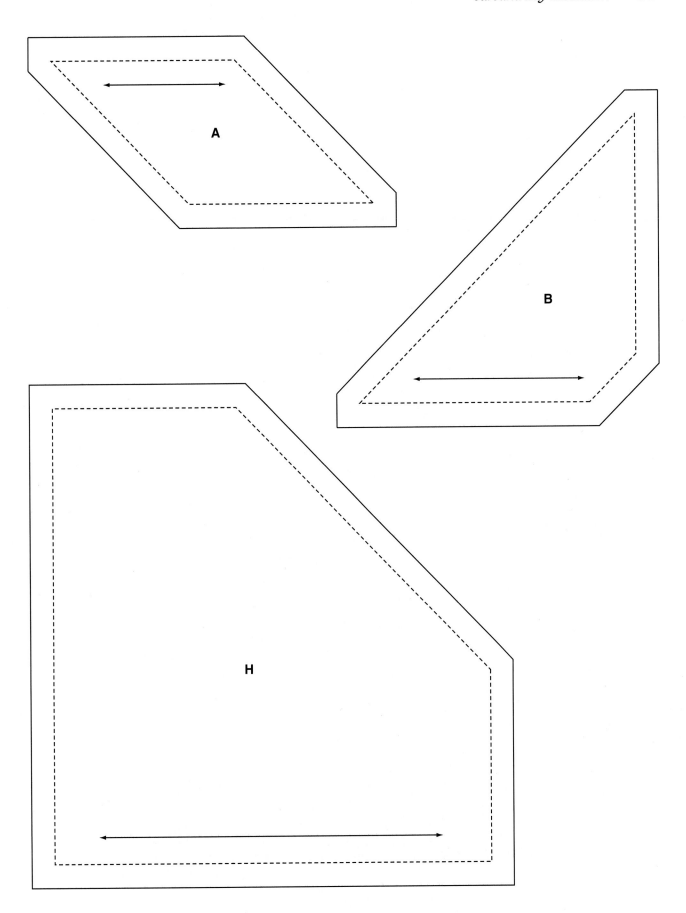

BLUE-AND-WHITE CHERRY BASKETS

Skill Level: *Intermediate*

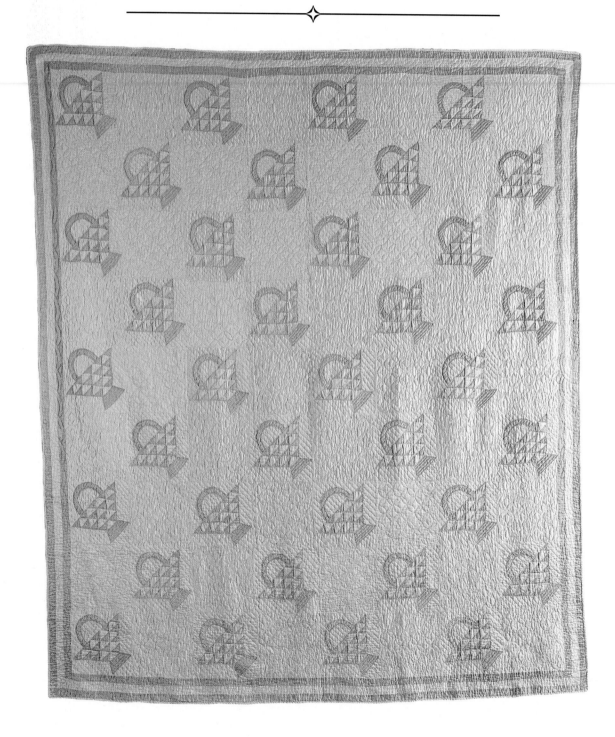

A delightful example of the popular blue-and-white color combination, this queen-size basket quilt offers much visual and tactile appeal. Its soft and satiny feel comes from the cotton sateen fabric used for both the quilt top and backing. This quilt was made in the 1920s by the grandmother of its current owner. While cotton sateen isn't used frequently today, this choice of fabric and pastel color was very popular with quilters between 1925 and 1950.

BEFORE YOU BEGIN

This basket is pieced from triangles, like several of the other basket blocks in this book. The bottom of the basket, however, is not made of a square and two triangles. Instead, it requires templates and set-in pieces. Prepare templates for pattern pieces A and B on page 58, referring to the directions on page 116 in "Quiltmaking Basics" for details on making templates. Note that you will need to cut one template B and one B reverse for each basket block. Use quick rotary-cutting techniques for the rest of the block pieces.

Quilt Sizes

	Queen (shown)	King
Finished Quilt Size	83" × 92½"	102" × 102"
Finished Block Size	9½"	9½"
Number of Basket Blocks	36	50
Number of Setting Squares	36	50

Materials

Fabric	Queen	King
Blue cotton sateen	3¾ yards	4⅞ yards
White cotton sateen	7¼ yards	10⅛ yards
Backing	7¾ yards	9⅜ yards
Batting	89" × 99"	108" × 108"
Binding	¾ yard	⅞ yard

NOTE: Yardages are based on 44/45-inch-wide fabrics that are at least 42 inches wide after preshrinking.

CHOOSING FABRICS

The quilt shown is made from just two fabrics: light blue sateen and white sateen. Sateen is a cotton fabric that has a slight sheen to it. It has a dressier, more elegant look and feel than regular cotton broadcloth. And unlike polished cottons, the satiny finish won't wash away when you preshrink your fabric. If you wish to use sateen for your quilt but can't find it at your local quilt shop, substitute blue and white broadcloth or inquire at a shop that sells dressmaking fabrics.

This quilt would look dramatically different if you deviated from the basic two-color scheme. To help see how it would look in a scrappy or multicolor scheme, photocopy the **Color Plan** on page 59, and use crayons or colored pencils to experiment with different color arrangements.

Cutting Chart

Fabric	Used For	Strip Width	Number of Strips	
			Queen	King
Blue	Baskets	24"	3	4
	Baskets	$2^3/8$"	6	9
	Basket bottoms	$4^1/2$"	3	4
	Borders	$1^1/2$"	17	20
White	Baskets	24"	3	4
	Baskets	$2^3/8$"	2	2
	Basket sides	$7^1/2$"	4	7
	Basket background	$8^3/8$"	4	5
	Bottom triangles	$3^3/4$"	2	3
	Setting squares	10"	9	13
	Border	$1^3/4$"	8	10

CUTTING

All measurements include $^1/4$-inch seam allowances. Refer to the cutting chart and cut strips in the width needed. Then cut those strips into pieces following the cutting directions that follow. All the blue pieces are listed first, followed by the white pieces. **Note:** Cut and piece one sample block before cutting all the pieces for the quilt.

Since all the baskets are made from the same two colors, we recommend that you use the grid technique to construct the blue-and-white triangle squares for the baskets. (For more on this, see "Piecing the Basket Blocks.") Use the 24-inch-wide strips cut from the blue and white fabrics for this technique, and use a $2^3/8$-inch grid.

• For the individual triangles needed for the basket, cut the $2^3/8$-inch-wide blue strips into $2^3/8$-inch squares. Cut each square in half diagonally, as shown in **Diagram 1.** Cut 90 squares for the queen-size quilt and 125 squares for the king size.

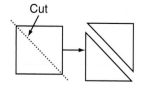

Diagram 1

• For the basket botttoms, cut 36 of template A for the queen-size quilt and 50 of template A for the king size from the $4^1/2$-inch-wide blue strips.

• For the basket handles, see page 110 in "Basket Basics" for information on preparing bias strips. Each basket needs a 1 × 11-inch bias strip that finishes to $^3/4$ inch. Cut enough 1-inch-wide bias strips to give you 396 inches for the queen-size quilt and 550 inches for the king size.

• For the individual white triangles needed for the basket, cut the $2^3/8$-inch-wide white strips into $2^3/8$-inch squares. Cut each square in half diagonally, as shown in **Diagram 1.** Cut 18 squares for the queen-size quilt and 25 squares for the king size.

• For each basket, cut two B pieces for the sides from the $4^1/2$-inch white strips. Lay two strips right sides together and press. Trace template B and cut it from both layers for one B and one B reverse.

• For the basket background, cut the $8^3/8$-inch-wide strips into $8^3/8$-inch squares. Cut the squares in half diagonally, as shown in **Diagram 1.**

• For the bottom triangles of the basket block, cut the $3^3/4$-inch-wide white strips into $3^3/4$-inch squares. Cut the squares in half diagonally.

• For the setting squares, cut the 10-inch-wide white strips into 10-inch squares. Cut 36 squares for the queen-size quilt and 50 for the king size.

PIECING THE BASKET BLOCKS

Hundreds of blue-and-white triangle squares are needed to complete this quilt. The grid technique explained on page 106 in "Basket Basics" allows you to assemble accurate triangle squares more quickly than you could using traditional piecing methods. Refer to the cutting chart for the total number of 24-inch blue and white strips required for your quilt. Cut each strip in half so you have pieces that measure approximately 21 × 24 inches. It will be easier to work with half-width strips. Mark these strips with a 2⅜-inch grid. For the queen-size quilt, you need a total of 324 triangle squares; for the king size, you need 450.

Step 1. Each basket contains five blue triangles, one white triangle, and nine blue-and-white triangle squares. Arrange and sew the triangle squares and triangles into five rows, as shown in **Diagram 2**. Press the seams in adjoining rows in opposite directions, then sew rows together, matching seams carefully.

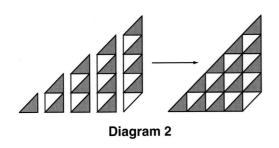

Diagram 2

Step 2. Sew a blue basket bottom A to the bottom of the partially completed basket unit, as shown in **Diagram 3**, stitching only between the dots, as indicated on template A.

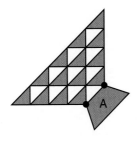

Diagram 3

Step 3. Sew a white piece B to the basket, as shown in **Diagram 4**, pivoting and setting in the seam where indicated by the dot. Press. Repeat on the opposite side, using the B reverse piece.

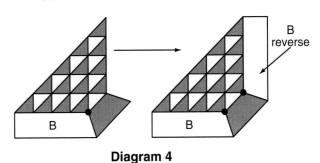

Diagram 4

Step 4. Center and sew a 3¾-inch white triangle to the bottom of the basket, as shown in **Diagram 5**. Press the seam toward the triangle.

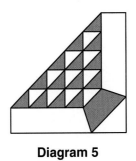

Diagram 5

Step 5. To make the handle for the basket, appliqué a 1 × 11-inch bias strip to an 8⅜-inch white basket background triangle using a blind stitch or other stitch of your choice. You will find complete instructions for constructing and appliquéing handles on page 110 in "Basket Basics."

Step 6. Sew the basket bottom to the handle triangle to complete the basket, as shown in the **Block Diagram.**

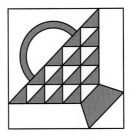

Block Diagram

Step 7. Repeat Steps 1 through 6 to make the number of basket blocks required for your quilt.

ASSEMBLING THE QUILT TOP

Step 1. Arrange your basket blocks and setting squares in rows, as shown in the **Assembly Diagram.** If you are making the king-size quilt, note that your quilt will be ten rows long by ten blocks wide.

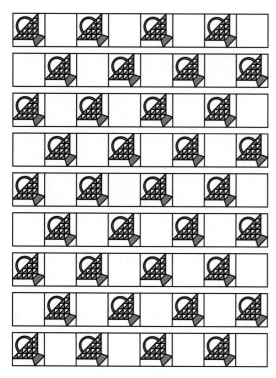

Assembly Diagram

Step 2. Sew the blocks together into rows, pressing the seams toward the setting squares. Sew the rows together, matching seams carefully. Press the seams between rows in one direction.

ADDING THE BORDERS

The quilt shown has three borders: an inner and outer narrow blue border and a middle white

border, which is slightly wider than the blue borders. Refer to the cutting chart for the number of strips required for the borders, then sew strips together end to end to achieve the lengths determined in the following steps.

Step 1. Measure the width of the quilt top through the horizontal center of the quilt rather than along the top or bottom. Make two border strips this exact length from the 1½-inch-wide blue strips.

Step 2. Fold one border strip in half crosswise and crease. Unfold it and position it right side down along the top edge of the quilt, with the crease at the vertical midpoint. Pin at the midpoint and ends first, then along the entire width of the quilt, easing in fullness if necessary. Sew the border to the quilt using a ¼-inch seam allowance. Press the seam toward the border. Repeat on the other end of the quilt.

Step 3. Measure the length of the quilt, taking the measurement through the vertical center of the quilt and including the top and bottom borders. Sew 1½-inch-wide blue border strips together to obtain two borders this exact length.

Step 4. Fold one strip in half crosswise and crease. Unfold it and position it right side down along one side of the quilt top, with the crease at the horizontal midpoint. Pin at the midpoint and ends first, then along the entire length of the quilt, easing in fullness if necessary. Stitch, using a ¼-inch seam allowance. Repeat on the opposite side of the quilt.

Step 5. In the same manner as for the inner border, piece together the 1¾-inch-wide white border strips. Measure and sew the borders to the quilt top, adding the top and bottom borders first, then the side borders.

Step 6. Use the additional 1½-inch-wide blue border strips to construct and sew the outer borders to the quilt. Measure in the same manner, including all borders in your measurements. The **Quilt Diagram** shows all three borders added.

Quilt Diagram

QUILTING AND FINISHING

Step 1. Mark the top for quilting, if desired. The quilt shown was outline quilted around the baskets. The basket backgrounds were quilted with parallel diagonal lines. The setting squares were quilted with a teacup design, and the borders were quilted with overlapping fans.

Step 2. Regardless of which quilt size you've chosen to make, the backing will have to be pieced. **Diagram 6** on page 58 illustrates the layout for both quilt backs. For the queen-size quilt, divide the backing fabric crosswise into three equal pieces, and trim the selvages. Cut a 31-inch-wide strip from each of two segments, then sew a

The teacup quilting design takes its name, aptly enough, from the kitchenware that resourceful quilters have used over the years to trace patterns of overlapping circles. Check your cupboard for a teacup or any other size cup with the diameter that suits the size pattern you want. Or make a circle from cardboard or template plastic.

31-inch-wide piece to each side of the remaining wide segment, as shown. Press the seams open.

Step 3. For the king-size quilt, divide the backing fabric crosswise into three equal pieces, and trim the selvages. Sew the three segments together along their long sides, as shown in **Diagram 6.** Press the seams open.

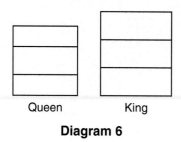

Queen   King

Diagram 6

Step 4. Layer the quilt top, batting, and backing, and baste the layers together. Quilt as desired.

Step 5. Referring to the directions on page 121 in "Quiltmaking Basics," make and attach double-fold binding. To calculate the amount of binding needed for the quilt size you are making, add the length of the four sides of the quilt and add 9 inches. The total is the approximate number of inches of binding you will need.

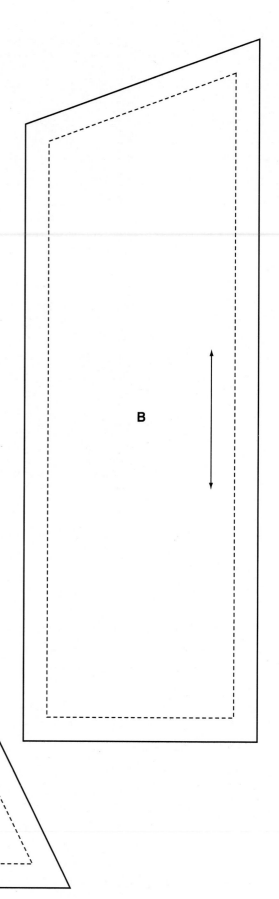

B

A

BLUE-AND-WHITE CHERRY BASKETS
Color Plan

Photocopy this page and use it to experiment with color schemes for your quilt.

Scrap Baskets with Nine-Patch Sashing

Skill Level: *Intermediate*

T his new quilt is fashioned in the tradional Grape Basket pattern. While this quilt has the look of a scrap quilt, the maker used a controlled palette of blues, burgundies, roses, peaches, and browns. You could expand upon the number of colors and patterns with successful results since the Nine-Patch sashing unifies the quilt with its secondary design.

BEFORE YOU BEGIN

Each basket handle requires several triangle squares. Directions are given for cutting triangles from squares to make the number needed of each scrap fabric. If you choose to make all of your baskets from either the same or a limited number of print fabrics, the grid technique explained on page 106 in "Basket Basics" will help you to construct triangle squares more quickly than you could using traditional methods. Use a $2^{7}/_{8}$-inch grid. Also note that the bias edge of the setting triangles will be the outside edge of your quilt. Handle these triangles carefully to avoid stretching them out of shape.

CHOOSING FABRICS

What could be more fun than raiding a scrap basket to make this delightful quilt? Mixing and matching colors and prints, darks and lights, and old fabrics and new can spark your imagination. If you don't have a scrap stash, buy lots of fat quarters in a wide variety of shades and patterns.

Of course, you can make this basket pattern in a limited color palette, too. Choose one color for the background, one for the baskets, and another for the sashing strips and Nine-Patch blocks. To help you create your own color scheme, photocopy the **Color Plan** on page 67, and use crayons or colored pencils to experiment with different color arrangements.

Quilt Sizes

	Double (shown)	Queen
Finished Quilt Size	$81^{1}/_{8}$" × $98^{1}/_{2}$"	$98^{1}/_{2}$" × $98^{1}/_{2}$"
Finished Block Size		
Basket	10"	10"
Nine Patch	$2^{1}/_{4}$"	$2^{1}/_{4}$"
Number of Blocks		
Basket	32	41
Nine Patch	49	60

Materials

	Double	Queen
Assorted prints	Approx. 12" × 13" of 32 prints *or* $1^{3}/_{4}$ yards total	Approx. 12" × 13" of 41 prints *or* $2^{1}/_{4}$ yards total
Muslin	$5^{3}/_{4}$ yards	7 yards
Blue print	$1^{3}/_{8}$ yards	$1^{5}/_{8}$ yards
Backing	$7^{5}/_{8}$ yards	$8^{5}/_{8}$ yards
Batting	88" × 105"	105" × 105"
Binding	$3/_{4}$ yard	$3/_{4}$ yard

NOTE: Yardages are based on 44/45-inch-wide fabrics that are at least 42 inches wide after preshrinking.

Cutting Chart

Fabric	Used For	Strip Width	Number of Strips Double	Number of Strips Queen
Assorted prints	Basket handles	2⅞"	1 of each	1 of each
	Basket feet	2⅞"	1 of each	1 of each
	Baskets	6⅞"	1 of each	1 of each
Muslin	Basket handles	2⅞"	8	11
	Basket background	6⅞"	3	4
	Basket sides	2½"	11	14
	Bottom triangles	4⅞"	2	3
	Sashing strips	1¼"	40	50
	Nine-Patch blocks	1¼"	6	8
	Setting triangles	15⅜"	2	2
	Outer border	4"	8	8
Blue print	Sashing strips	1¼"	20	25
	Nine-Patch blocks	1¼"	8	10
	Inner border	1¼"	8	8

NOTE: Strip widths are assumed to be 42 inches except for the assorted print fabrics for the baskets, which are assumed to be 12 inches wide based on the fabric requirement given in the Materials chart.

CUTTING

All pieces are cut using rotary-cutting techniques. Refer to the Cutting Chart and cut the required number of strips in the width needed. Cut all strips across the fabric width. From these strips, subcut the individual pieces according to the instructions provided here. All measurements include ¼-inch seam allowances.

• For the basket handles, cut the 2⅞-inch-wide assorted print and muslin strips into 2⅞-inch squares. Cut the squares in half diagonally, as shown in **Diagram 1**.

• For the basket feet, cut the 2⅞-inch print strips into 2⅞-inch squares. Cut the squares in half diagonally.

• For the baskets, cut one 6⅞-inch square from each print. Cut the square in half diagonally. You need one triangle per basket.

• For the basket background, cut the 6⅞-inch muslin strips into 6⅞-inch squares. You need 16 squares for the double size and 21 squares for the queen size; cut all squares in half diagonally.

• For the basket sides, cut the 2½-inch-wide muslin strips into 2½ × 6½-inch rectangles. Cut two for each block.

• For the bottom triangles of the basket blocks, cut the 4⅞-inch-wide muslin strips into 4⅞-inch squares. Cut 16 for the double-size quilt and 21 for the queen size. Cut the squares in half diagonally.

• For the side setting triangles, cut the 15⅜-inch-wide muslin strips into two 15⅜-inch squares. Cut the squares diagonally both ways, as shown in **Diagram 1**.

• For the corner setting triangles, cut two 8-inch squares from the leftover 15⅜-inch muslin strips. Cut each square in half diagonally.

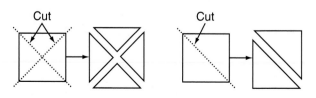

Diagram 1

PIECING THE BASKET BLOCKS

Step 1. Seven identical triangle squares are needed to complete the handle of each basket. Use four 2$\frac{7}{8}$-inch squares from the assorted prints and four from muslin. Draw a diagonal line on one side of each muslin square, then pair each square with its print counterpart, with right sides together. Match edges of pairs carefully, then sew a seam $\frac{1}{4}$ inch from each side of the drawn line. After sewing the seams, cut the squares in half on the drawn line. Press the seam in each resulting triangle square toward the blue fabric. See **Diagram 2.**

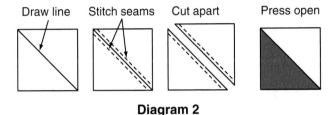

Diagram 2

This method produces eight triangle squares, one extra than you need for each basket. If you are repeating print fabrics, just use the extra in another block. If you are not repeating fabrics, sew only one seam on one pair. When cut apart, you will have one triangle square plus a muslin and print 2$\frac{7}{8}$-inch triangle. The print triangle can be used to make the foot of the basket.

Step 2. Sew the triangle squares together into two units, referring to **Diagram 3** for placement. Press the seams toward the print fabric.

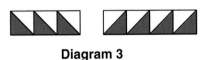

Diagram 3

Step 3. Each block requires two 6$\frac{7}{8}$-inch triangles—one muslin and one print. Sew the short triangle-square unit to the muslin triangle, as shown in **Diagram 4.** Press the seam toward the muslin. Then sew the longer triangle-square unit to the muslin triangle as shown, matching seams where the triangle squares meet. Press.

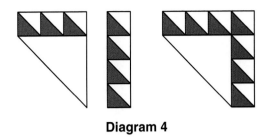

Diagram 4

Step 4. Sew the print triangle to the bottom of unit, as shown in **Diagram 5.** Press the seam toward the print triangle.

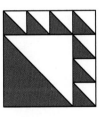

Diagram 5

Step 5. Sew a 2$\frac{7}{8}$-inch print triangle to one end of two 2$\frac{1}{2} \times 6\frac{1}{2}$-inch muslin rectangles, as shown in **Diagram 6.**

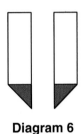

Diagram 6

Step 6. Sew the rectangle units to the partially assembled basket, as shown in **Diagram 7.** Press the seams toward the print fabric. (If seams are too bulky, press them toward the muslin.)

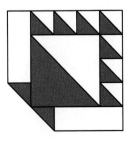

Diagram 7

Step 7. Sew a 4⅞-inch muslin triangle to the bottom of the basket, as shown in the **Block Diagram,** completing the block. Press the seam toward the print fabric. Repeat to make the number of basket blocks required for your quilt.

Block Diagram

MAKING THE SASHING STRIPS

Step 1. Refer to the cutting chart for the number of 1¼ × 42-inch strips of muslin and blue print fabric required for your quilt. Pin and sew a muslin strip to each side of a blue print strip, as shown in **Diagram 8.** Press the seams toward the blue strip.

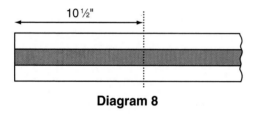

Diagram 8

Step 2. Square up one end of a set, then cut as many 10½-inch segments as possible from the long strip set. Make 80 sashing strips for the double-size quilt and 100 for the queen-size quilt.

PIECING THE NINE-PATCH BLOCKS

The Nine-Patch blocks can be assembled quickly using strip-piecing techniques. The dark portions of sashing, the inner border, and the binding are all sewn from the same fabric.

Step 1. Pin and sew a blue print Nine-Patch strip to either side of a muslin Nine-Patch strip to make strip set A, as shown in **Diagram 9.** Press the seams toward the print strips. Square up one end of the strip set, then cut as many 1¼-inch segments from it as possible.

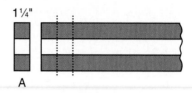

Diagram 9

Sew Easy

If your strips ripple when making the sashing strips and Nine-Patch blocks, start sewing the third strip at the end where your first seam stopped. Match edges carefully and pin strips before sewing. If you still have distortion problems, shorten the length of your strip units to about 22 inches, since shorter lengths are somewhat easier to handle.

Step 2. Pin and sew a muslin Nine-Patch strip to either side of a blue print Nine-Patch strip to make strip set B. Press seams toward the blue strip. This strip set will look just like the strip sets you made for the sashing strips (see **Diagram 8**). Square up one end of the strip set, then cut as many 1¼-inch segments from it as possible.

Step 3. Sew an A segment to the top and bottom of a B segment, as shown in **Diagram 10,** matching seams carefully. Repeat until you have assembled 49 Nine-Patch blocks for the double size and 60 Nine-Patch blocks for the queen size.

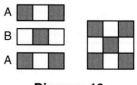

Diagram 10

If you have leftover pieces from the sashing strips that weren't quite 10½ inches long, you can use them for the Nine-Patch blocks. Simply cut 1¼-inch B segments from each leftover strip set.

ASSEMBLING THE QUILT TOP

Step 1. Use a design wall or flat surface to lay out the basket blocks, setting triangles, sashing strips, and Nine-Patch blocks in diagonal rows. The double-size quilt is shown in the **Assembly Diagram**. For the queen-size quilt, your layout will be one block wider.

Step 2. Sew the rows of basket blocks and sashing strips together exactly as shown, pressing seams toward the sashing strips. Notice that the fourth diagonal row has a sashing strip

Assembly Diagram

sewn to the top and bottom of the basket row. These rows must be sewn together as a unit before the setting triangles will fit. Sew the remaining rows of sashing strips and Nine-Patch blocks together, pressing seams toward the sashing strips.

Step 3. Sew the side setting triangles to the ends of the basket block rows. Sew all rows together. Sew the corner setting triangles on last. Press.

Note: The larger quilt is assembled in much the same manner; however, some rows will contain a different number of blocks.

ADDING THE BORDERS

The quilt has a narrow blue print inner border and a wider muslin outer border, as shown in the **Quilt Diagram** on page 66. You will sew the border strips for each side together first, then add them to the quilt top as a single unit, mitering the corners. See page 119 in "Quiltmaking Basics" for details on adding borders with mitered corners.

Step 1. To determine the correct length for the side borders, measure the quilt top vertically through the center. To this measurement add two times the finished width of the double border (3½ inches + 1 inch = 4½ inches) plus 5 inches. This is the length you need to make the two side borders. In the same manner, measure the quilt top horizontally through the center, then calculate the length of the top and bottom borders.

Step 2. Sew the print border strips together end to end until you've achieved the required lengths for each border. Repeat with the muslin border strips. Be sure to keep the side border strips separate from the top and bottom border strips if you're making the double-size quilt. For the queen-size quilt, the border lengths will be the same for the sides, top, and bottom.

Step 3. Working with the side border strips first, pin and sew the long strips together lengthwise into two units. Press seams toward the outer border. In the same manner, pin and sew the top and bottom border strips together into two units. Press seams toward the outer border.

Step 4. Pin and sew the four border units to the quilt top, carefully lining up the matching strips in adjacent borders.

QUILTING AND FINISHING

Step 1. Mark the top for quilting, if desired.

Step 2. Regardless of which quilt size you've chosen to make, the backing will have to be pieced. **Diagram 11** illustrates the layout for either the double- or queen-size quilt back. For either quilt, divide the backing fabric crosswise into three equal pieces, and trim the selvages. Sew the three pieces together along the long sides, and press the seams open.

Diagram 11

Step 3. Layer the quilt top, batting, and backing, and baste the layers together. Quilt as desired.

Step 4. Referring to the directions on page 121 in "Quiltmaking Basics," make and attach double-fold binding with a finished width of ½ inch. Add the length of the four sides of the quilt plus 9 inches. The total is the approximate number of inches of binding you will need.

Quilt Diagram

SCRAP BASKETS WITH NINE-PATCH SASHING

Color Plan

Photocopy this page and use it to experiment with color schemes for your quilt.

Red-and-Green Appliquéd Baskets

Skill Level: *Challenging*

*T*his unusual twin-size appliquéd quilt dates back to the 1860s or 1870s. Both the colors and the quilting patterns help to identify the era in which this stunning combination of precision piecing and whimsical appliqué was stitched. It is made entirely of cotton, and the very close lines of stitching not only help to hold the cotton batting in place but also form an interesting ribbonlike visual effect that has become more pronounced with age.

BEFORE YOU BEGIN

This quilt combines both piecing and appliquéing; patterns are provided on pages 74–76. Make templates for each piece, referring to "Quiltmaking Basics" for complete details on making and using templates.

The quilt shown has unusual borders. A strip border is sewn to the top, bottom, and right side, while an appliquéd border is attached to the two sides and the bottom. Yardage requirements allow enough fabric to add strip and appliquéd borders to all sides of your quilt, if desired.

CHOOSING FABRICS

The quilt in the photograph was made from three solid colors and a white background. Although the colors have faded over the years, it is still evident that a very bright green was used, along with red and a lighter shade of green, which now appears almost yellow.

If red and green are not for you, try making this quilt from any three complementary colors. Or use a large variety of colors for the appliquéd border blossoms. It may even be fun to make the border from scraps, tying the whole color scheme together with a specific-color basket or large blossom combination.

To help develop your own unique color scheme for the quilt, photocopy the **Color Plan** on page 77, and use crayons or colored pencils to experiment with different color arrangements.

Quilt Size	
Finished Quilt Size	69½" × 87¼"
Finished Block Size	17"
Number of Basket Blocks	6

NOTE: Due to the complexity of the design, no size variations are given.

Materials	
Fabric	**Amount**
Muslin	5¾ yards
Bright green	3 yards
Red	1 yard
Light green	2 yards
Backing	5¾ yards
Batting	76" × 94"
Binding	¾ yard

NOTE: Yardages are based on 44/45-inch wide fabrics that are at least 42 inches wide after preshrinking.

Cutting Chart

Fabric	Used For	Strip Width or Piece	Number to Cut
Muslin	Background and setting squares	17½"	4
	Side and corner setting triangles	25¼"	2
	Border	9½"	7
Bright green	Large blossom	A	84
	Large leaves	G	24
	Large leaves	G reverse	24
	Small leaves	H	12
	Small leaves	H reverse	12
	Basket	C	6
	Border blossom	I	18
	Border blossom	J	18
	Border leaf	N	20
	Border leaf	N reverse	20
	Border	1½"	7
Red	Large blossom	A	60
	Large blossom	B	6
	Basket	D	6
	Small blossom	E	12
	Border blossom	L	18
	Border blossom	M	18
	Border	1½"	7
Light green	Large blossom	A	24
	Small blossom	F	12
	Border blossom	K	18

CUTTING

The measurements for the background blocks, setting squares, and borders include ¼-inch seam allowances. Referring to the Cutting Chart, cut the required number of strips in the width needed. Cut all strips across the fabric width (crosswise grain).

For the background and setting squares, cut the 17½-inch-wide strips into eight 17½-inch squares. For the side setting triangles, cut the 25¼-inch-wide strips into two 25¼-inch squares. Cut each square diagonally both ways, as shown in **Diagram 1**. From the remainder of the 25¼-inch strips, cut two 12⅞-inch squares. Cut each square in half diagonally one way for the corner setting triangles.

Referring to the Cutting Chart, cut the number of each appliqué piece required. Add seam allowances when cutting the pieces from the fabric.

You will also need to make approximately 600 inches of ½-inch finished bias for the stems and border vines. Refer to page 110 in "Basket Basics" for directions on cutting and making bias strips.

Note: Cut and stitch one sample block before cutting all the fabric for the quilt.

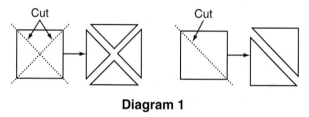

Diagram 1

PIECING THE LARGE BLOSSOMS

Step 1. Each large blossom is made from four wedge-shaped pieces and a bottom strip, as indicated by the heavy outlines on **Diagram 2**. To make four wedges, lay out the bright green, red, and light green A diamonds into rows, as shown in **Diagram 3**. Sew the diamonds into rows and press the seams toward the red diamonds. Sew the rows together, as shown, matching seams carefully. End each seam ¼ inch from the bright green edge. This will help you turn under the edge when you prepare the blossom for appliqué. Press the seams open. Repeat to make a total of four wedge units.

Step 2. Referring again to **Diagram 2**, sew the four units together as shown, matching seams carefully as you work and pressing as you go. Sew the two left units together and the two right units together before joining the center seam. If your blossom is slightly out of shape due to the many bias edges of the diamonds, gently pull as you press to square up the blossom. Steam the blossom and allow it to dry before handling.

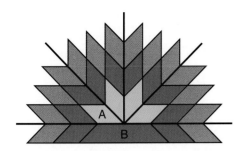

Diagram 2

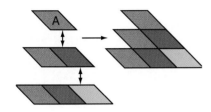

Diagram 3

Step 3. Sew a red A diamond to either short end of the red B shape. Sew a bright green A diamond to the outer ends to complete the lower row of petals, as shown in **Diagram 4**. Press the seams in the lower row in the direction opposite those they will join in the upper unit, then sew the two sections together (see **Diagram 2**). Remember to start and stop the seam ¼ inch from each end.

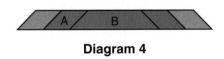

Diagram 4

Step 4. Turn the outer edges under ¼ inch and baste in place. Refer to page 107 in "Basket Basics" for information on preparing points and corners for appliqué.

Step 5. Repeat Steps 1 through 4 to make a total of six large blossoms. Set them aside while you construct the remaining pieces for each block.

APPLIQUÉING THE BLOCKS

Step 1. Prepare the C and D basket pieces, the small E and F blossom pieces, and the G, G reverse,

H, and H reverse leaf pieces for your favorite method of appliqué. You need one basket, one large blossom, two small blossoms, four small leaves (two are reverse), and eight large leaves (four are reverse) for each block.

Step 2. Fold a 17½-inch muslin square diagonally and finger press. Fold along the other diagonal and finger press. Fold vertically, then horizontally, finger pressing each time. The folds divide the block into visual segments, which will help you position the appliqué pieces symmetrically.

Step 3. Referring to the **Block Diagram** and the photograph on page 68, position the basket and blossom pieces on the muslin squares.

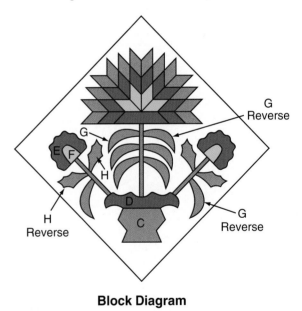

Block Diagram

Step 4. Center and pin the large blossom in the upper portion of the block, then position the two basket pieces beneath it, with the basket rim overlapping the raw edge of the top of the basket. Leave approximately 7 inches between the bottom of the large blossom and the rim of the basket (the length of your finished stem). Be sure to avoid placing appliqué pieces within the ¼-inch seam allowance surrounding the block.

Step 5. Cut a 7½-inch length from your bright green bias stem. Position it between the basket and large flower, tucking its raw edges under the

at each end. Pin three large leaves on each side of the stem (see the **Block Diagram** on page 71).

Step 6. Cut two 5¹⁄₂-inch lengths from the bright green bias stem. Position and pin these at about a 45 degree angle from the outer edge of the basket rim. Pin a small blossom at the top end of each stem, overlapping the stem by about ¹⁄₄ inch.

Step 7. Pin a small leaf on each side of the short stems and a large leaf on the outside edge of the stem. See the **Block Diagram** on page 71. Tuck the unfinished leaf ends under the stem.

Step 8. Take a look at your block. Rearrange any pieces as necessary to make a pleasing arrangement. When you are satisfied with the appearance of the block, appliqué each piece using a blind stitch and matching thread.

Step 9. Repeat Steps 1 through 8 to make a total of six basket blocks. Use your first block as a placement guide for the pieces in remaining blocks.

ASSEMBLING THE QUILT TOP

Step 1. Lay out and sew basket blocks, setting squares, side setting triangles, and corner setting triangles into diagonal rows, as shown in the **Assembly Diagram.** Press the seams toward the setting squares and triangles.

Step 2. Sew the rows together. Press.

ADDING THE STRIP BORDERS

Narrow red and bright green borders are sewn to the top, bottom, and right side of the quilt before the appliquéd borders are added. If you prefer to add these borders to all sides of your quilt, cut extra strips of each color and add them now before the appliquéd borders are measured and added.

Step 1. Measure the quilt length through the vertical center rather than along the sides. Sew the 1¹⁄₂-inch-wide red strips together end to end to make one (or two) borders this exact length. Repeat with the 1¹⁄₂-inch-wide bright green strips.

Assembly Diagram

Step 2. Pin and sew the red and green border strips together lengthwise. Press the seam toward the red strip. Repeat with the remaining pair if you are adding a strip border unit to both sides.

Step 3. Fold a border strip in half crosswise and crease. Unfold it and position the red end of the strip right side down along the right side of your quilt, with the crease at the horizontal midpoint. Pin at the midpoint and ends first, then across the length of the quilt, easing in fullness if necessary. Sew the border unit to the quilt. Press the seam toward the border. Sew another border unit to the left side of the quilt, if desired.

Step 4. Repeat Steps 1 through 3 to make top and bottom borders in the same manner. Measure the width of the quilt through the horizontal center of the quilt and include all side borders to determine the length needed for the top and bottom borders.

ADDING THE APPLIQUÉD BORDERS

Like the strip borders, the appliquéd borders appear only on three sides of the quilt shown. To make appliquéd borders on all sides of your quilt, cut extra muslin border strips and enough appliqué pieces to continue the motif around the quilt.

Step 1. Piece the 9½-inch-wide muslin border strips to obtain one (or two) strip the width of the quilt for the bottom (and top) of the quilt. Piece two more strips to the measurement of the length of the quilt plus the width of the bottom (and top) appliqué border.

Step 2. Prepare pieces I through N for appliqué. Refer to the Cutting Chart on page 70 for the number of pieces you need.

Step 3. Refer to the **Quilt Diagram** on page 74 for placement of the border appliqué pieces. The green bias strip has four deep curves on the bottom of the quilt and seven curves on the sides. A pair of blossoms is at the center of each curve, with leaves spaced along the stem between them. The side borders are mirror images of each other.

Pin a length of green bias vine to the border as shown, forming curves. Pin blossoms in the center of curves, tucking their bright green stems under the vine. The light green base of each blossom is positioned under the red portion of the blossom. Check placement on all sides to make sure your pieces will not be lost in a seam allowance.

Sew Easy

When making appliquéd borders, add an extra inch to the calculated length of the borders. Doing so will allow you to square up the ends after your appliqué is complete, eliminating the distortion that can take place during sewing and handling. When positioning pieces, keep in mind that design elements within ¾ to 1 inch of the border ends will be either trimmed away or sewn in the seams.

Step 4. When you are satisfied with the appearance of the border, appliqué each piece in place using a blind stitch and matching thread.

Step 5. Assemble the remaining appliquéd borders.

Step 6. Sew the bottom border to the quilt, using the same method as for the pieced narrow strip border. Trim the border to the correct length before sewing it, centering design elements. If you have made a top border, sew that to the quilt now.

Step 7. Sew the side borders to the quilt in the same manner as you did for the bottom border.

QUILTING AND FINISHING

Step 1. Mark the quilt top for quilting. The quilt shown was heavily quilted in a crosshatch pattern with lines about ½ inch apart.

Step 2. To piece the quilt back, first cut the backing fabric crosswise into two equal pieces, and trim the selvages. Cut one of the segments in half lengthwise, and sew one half to each side of the full-width piece, as shown in **Diagram 5.** Press the seams open.

Step 3. Layer the backing, batting, and quilt top; baste. Quilt as desired.

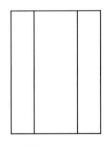

Diagram 5

Step 4. Referring to the directions on page 121 in "Quiltmaking Basics," make and attach double-fold binding. Add the length of the four sides of the quilt plus 9 inches to calculate the number of inches of binding you will need.

Quilt Diagram

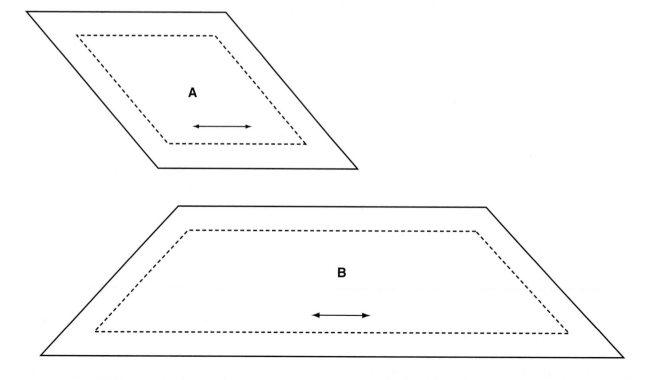

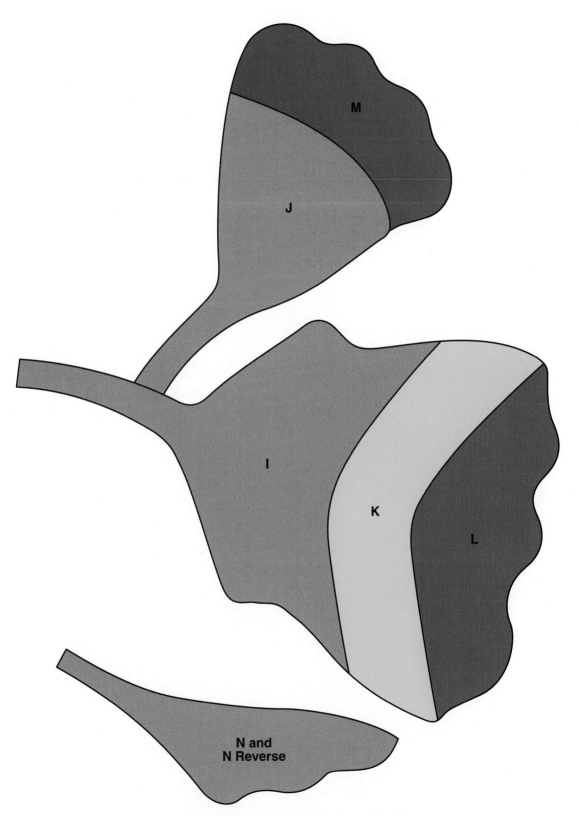

Appliqué Border Blossoms and Leaf

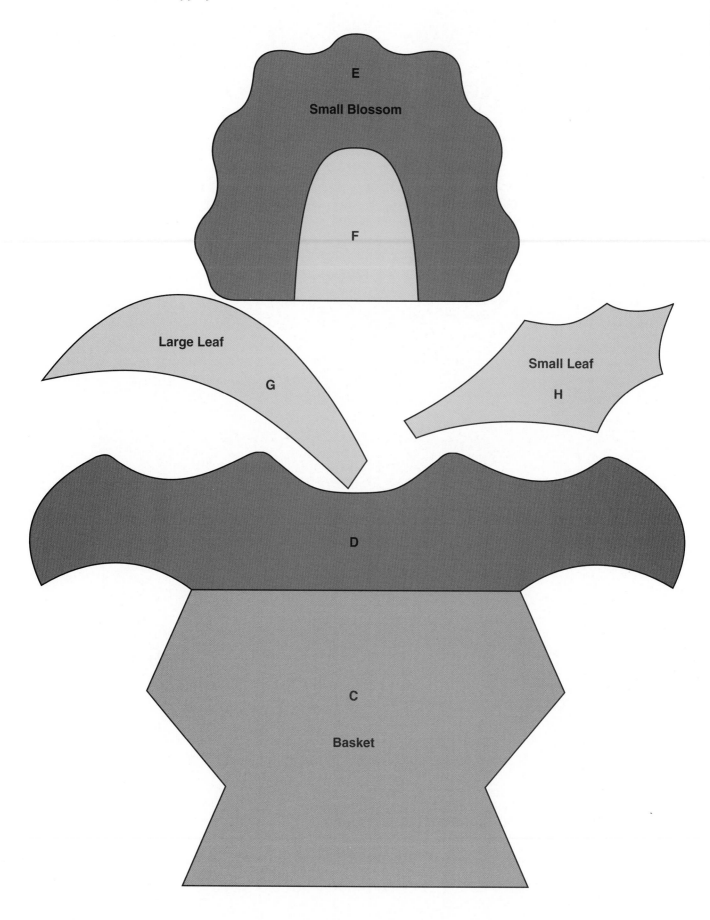

E

Small Blossom

F

Large Leaf

G

Small Leaf

H

D

C

Basket

Red-and-Green Appliquéd Baskets

Color Plan

Photocopy this page and use it to experiment with color schemes for your quilt.

AMISH-STYLE SCRAP BASKETS

Skill Level: *Intermediate*

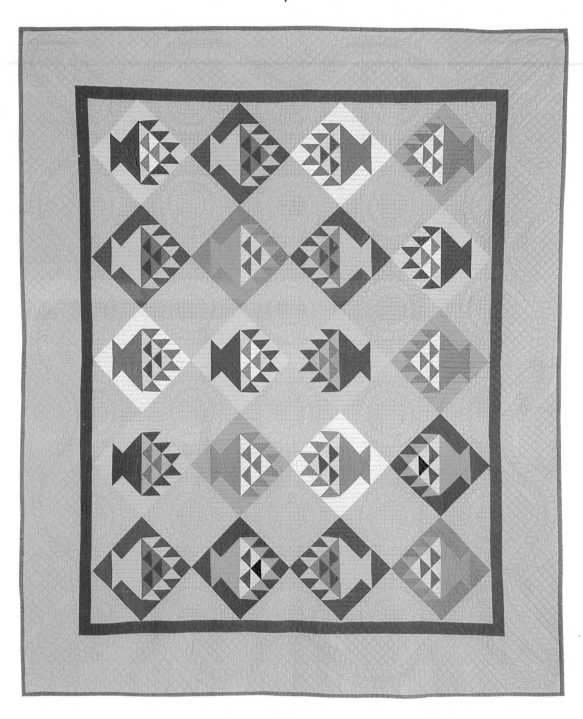

This Cake Stand Basket is filled with colorful fruit or flowers, whichever your imagination prefers. Made entirely of deep, rich, solid fabrics in the Amish tradition, this modern twin-size quilt was inspired by an antique. Even the quilting patterns are typical of the intricate wreaths and vines quilted so exquisitely by the Amish. Traditional cross-hatching provides a backdrop for the splendid feathered quilting and vibrant colors of the baskets.

BEFORE YOU BEGIN

The quilt shown in the photograph was stitched from a variety of solid fabrics in the Amish style. While the overall effect is that of a scrap quilt, each basket uses five colors. One color is used for the basket, one color is for the background, and three contrasting colors are for the basket's contents. To simplify the yardage and cutting charts, directions are given as though all baskets are cut from the same five fabrics. However, if you plan to make a scrap quilt, you may substitute small pieces of different fabrics as long as your total yardage equals that given. An assortment of fat eighths and fat quarters would work well in providing variety for your quilt.

Quilt Sizes

	Twin (shown)	Queen
Finished Quilt Size	66" × 78½"	91" × 103½"
Finished Block Size	8¾"	8¾"
Number of Blocks	20	42

Materials

	Twin	Queen
Basket fabric	1 yard	1¾ yards
Basket background fabric	1¼ yards	2 yards
Three contrasting fabrics	⅜ yard *each*	¾ yard *each*
Light gray	3⅛ yards	5¼ yards
Burgundy	⅜ yard	⅝ yard
Backing	5 yards	8¼ yards
Batting	72" × 85"	97" × 110"
Binding	⅝ yard	⅞ yard

NOTE: *Yardages are based on 44/45-inch-wide fabrics that are at least 42 inches wide after preshrinking.*

CHOOSING FABRICS

This quilt combines many of the dark solid hues associated with Amish quilts: purple, burgundy, green, dark blue, and gray. Surprisingly, it contains no black, a color often found in Amish quilts. The color choices for blocks in this quilt appear to be almost randomly selected, yet several color combinations repeat, creating a subtle visual harmony. Whether the basket is dark or medium and the background bright or pale, the contrasting values of light, medium, and dark shades help your eyes dance over this delightful quilt.

To achieve a pleasing scrap look with some underlying unity, pick a basic color scheme as this

angles. Arrange and sew the three triangle squares from Step 5 with three of these triangles into rows, referring to **Diagram 5** for color placement. Save your extra triangle for your next block. Press the seams in adjoining rows in opposite directions, then sew rows together to form the basket contents.

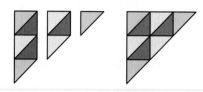

Diagram 5

Step 7. Sew the shorter handle unit to the side of the basket contents, as shown in **Diagram 6.**

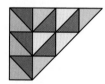

Diagram 6

Step 8. Now sew the remaining handle unit to the other side of basket contents, as shown in **Diagram 7.**

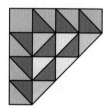

Diagram 7

Step 9. Sew a large basket fabric triangle to the bottom of the partially assembled basket, as shown in **Diagram 8.**

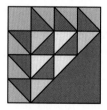

Diagram 8

Step 10. Sew a small basket fabric triangle to one end of two $2\frac{1}{4} \times 5\frac{3}{4}$-inch rectangles, referring to **Diagram 9** for placement. Press seams toward the darker fabric.

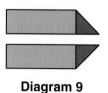

Diagram 9

Step 11. Sew the rectangle units to the partially completed basket block, as shown in **Diagram 10.** Press the seams toward the darker fabric.

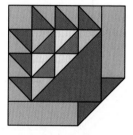

Diagram 10

Step 12. Sew a $4\frac{3}{8}$-inch bottom triangle to the bottom of the basket, as shown in the **Block Diagram,** completing the block. Press the seam toward the triangle.

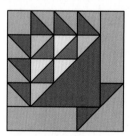

Block Diagram

Step 13. Repeat Steps 1 through 12 until you have assembled the number of blocks required for your quilt.

ASSEMBLING THE QUILT TOP

Step 1. Use a design wall or other flat surface to lay out the basket blocks, setting squares, side setting triangles, and corner setting triangles into diagonal rows, referring to the **Assembly Diagram.** For the queen-size quilt, your layout will be six baskets across by seven baskets down. Note that for either quilt, the baskets all point toward the vertical center of the quilt.

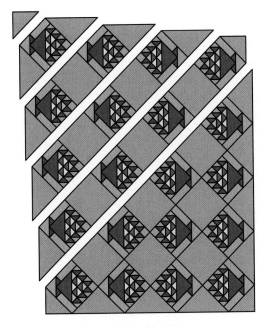

Assembly Diagram

Step 2. Once you are pleased with your block arrangement, sew the blocks and setting pieces together into rows. Press the seam allowances toward the setting squares and triangles. Sew the rows together, matching seams carefully. Press.

ADDING THE BORDERS

Step 1. For either size quilt, sew the 2-inch-wide inner border strips together end to end.

Step 2. Measure the width of the quilt top, taking the measurement through the horizontal center of the quilt rather than along the top or bottom. Cut two border strips to this exact length.

Step 3. Fold one border strip in half crosswise and crease. Unfold it and position it right side down along the top edge of the quilt, with the crease at the vertical midpoint. Pin at the midpoint and ends first, then along the length of the entire edge, easing in fullness if necessary. Sew the border to the quilt top using a 1/4-inch seam allowance. Press the seam allowance toward the border. Repeat on the other end of the quilt.

Step 4. Measure the length of the quilt, taking the measurement through the vertical center of the quilt and including the top and bottom borders. Cut the remaining long border strip to obtain two borders this exact length.

Step 5. Stitch the side borders to the quilt top as you did for the top and bottom borders, pinning at the midpoints and easing in fullness if necessary.

Step 6. In the same manner as for the inner border, piece together the 7-inch wide outer border strips. Measure and sew the borders to the quilt top, adding the top and bottom borders first, followed by the side borders. The completed twin-size quilt top should look like the one in the **Quilt Diagram** on page 84. If you are making the queen-size quilt, you will have more basket blocks, but the borders will be the same as for the twin-size quilt.

QUILTING AND FINISHING

Step 1. Mark the top for quilting. The quilt shown was quilted with vertical lines about 1/2 inch apart through each basket block. The setting squares were quilted with feathered wreaths and background cross-hatching. The setting triangles have half wreaths and cross-hatching. The borders were quilted with a feathered vine motif.

Step 2. Regardless of which quilt size you've chosen to make, the backing will have to be pieced. For the twin-size quilt, divide the 5 yards of backing fabric crosswise into two 2 1/2-yard pieces, and trim the selvages.

Step 3. Cut one of the pieces in half lengthwise, and sew one half to each side of the full-

Quilt Diagram

width piece, as shown in **Diagram 11**. Press the seams open.

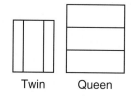

Twin   Queen

Diagram 11

Step 4. For the queen-size quilt, divide the 8$\frac{1}{3}$-yard length of fabric crosswise into three equal pieces, and trim the selvages.

Step 5. Sew the three pieces together along the long sides, as shown in **Diagram 11**, and press the seams open.

Step 6. Layer the quilt top, batting, and backing, and baste the layers together. Quilt as desired.

Step 7. Referring to the directions on page 121 in "Quiltmaking Basics," make and attach double-fold binding. To calculate the amount of binding needed for the quilt size you are making, add the lengths of the four sides of the quilt plus 9 inches. The total is the approximate number of inches of binding you will need.

Amish-Style Scrap Baskets
Color Plan

Photocopy this page and use it to experiment with color schemes for your quilt.

ANTIQUE LILY BASKETS
Skill Level: *Intermediate*

*T*his antique twin-size quilt from Indiana was most likely stitched in the 1880s. Two shades of the then-popular double pink fabric are used throughout, along with brown baskets and a yellow miniprint, which all help to date this unsigned quilt. The Lily Baskets are very traditional, yet the quiltmaker saw fit to liven them up with Streak of Lightning borders that add a bit of fun to the overall design.

BEFORE YOU BEGIN

The baskets in this quilt are made from triangle squares with additional triangles added. Because the baskets are identical, we recommend you try the grid method of piecing triangle squares, described on page 106 in "Basket Basics." Note that in the cutting directions, we have given the number of strips to cut for triangles, should you prefer to use another method. These strip requirements are noted as optional, as you would not cut your fabric into strips to use the grid method.

This quilt also contains appliquéd lily blossoms. See page 108 in "Basket Basics" for information on appliqué techniques. You will need to make a template for the leaves (pattern A and A reverse on page 94).

CHOOSING FABRICS

The fabrics used in the quilt pictured were all the fashion in the 1880s. Today, you can make this quilt using fabrics in the same style and color scheme because many fabric companies are now manufacturing reproduction prints. Choose similar fabrics for an antique feel or make your own color statement using today's prints and colors.

You'll notice a difference in color in the background muslin fabric from the top part of the block to the baskets. You can choose to make all of the background pieces the same or try tea-dyed muslin for the darker look of the basket bottom.

To help you develop your own unique color scheme for the

Quilt Sizes

	Twin (shown)	Queen
Finished Quilt Size	74$^{1}/_{8}$" × 85$^{1}/_{2}$"	85$^{1}/_{2}$" × 116$^{7}/_{8}$"
Finished Block Size	15$^{1}/_{2}$"	15$^{1}/_{2}$"
Number of Blocks	12	20

Materials

	Twin	Queen
Unbleached muslin	1$^{1}/_{2}$ yards	2$^{3}/_{8}$ yards
Tan	3$^{1}/_{4}$ yards	3$^{1}/_{2}$ yards
Dark pink print	4$^{3}/_{8}$ yards	6$^{1}/_{2}$ yards
Brown print	1$^{1}/_{4}$ yards	1$^{3}/_{4}$ yards
Green	$^{1}/_{2}$ yard	$^{3}/_{4}$ yard
Yellow print	$^{3}/_{8}$ yard	$^{5}/_{8}$ yard
Medium pink print	$^{3}/_{8}$ yard	$^{5}/_{8}$ yard
Backing	5$^{3}/_{8}$ yards	8 yards
Batting	81" × 92"	92" × 123"
Binding	$^{3}/_{4}$ yard	$^{7}/_{8}$ yard

NOTE: Yardages are based on 44/45-inch-wide fabrics that are at least 42 inches wide after preshrinking.

Cutting Chart

Fabric	Used For	Strip Width	Number of Strips	
			Twin	Queen
Muslin	Background triangles	15⅞"	3	5
Tan	Basket block corner triangles	5⅞"	1	2
	Block sides	10⅞"	2	3
	Squares for baskets	3"	1	2
	Border triangles	4½"	6	6
	Basket triangles	25"	1	2
Dark pink	Setting squares*	15½"	1	1
	Side setting triangles*	22½"	1	1
	Corner setting triangles	11½"	1	1
	Border triangles	4½"	6	6
Brown print	Baskets	3⅜"	3	5
	Basket triangles	25"	1	2
Green solid	Flower bases	3"	2	3
	Stems	1"	2	3
	Leaves A		24	40
	Leaves A Reverse		24	40
Medium pink print	Flower petals	2½"	25	38
Yellow print	Flower petals	2½"	25	38

Cut these strips lengthwise. Cut a 115-inch length for the twin-size quilt and a 190-inch length for the queen size.

quilt, photocopy the **Color Plan** on page 95, and use crayons or colored pencils to experiment with different color arrangements.

CUTTING

The measurements for the background blocks, setting squares, and borders include ¼-inch seam allowances. Referring to the Cutting Chart, cut the required number of strips in the width needed. Cut all strips across the fabric width (crosswise grain), except for the dark pink print fabric. Cut a 115-inch *lengthwise* strip for the twin-size quilt and a 190-inch *lengthwise* strip for the queen-size quilt. For either size quilt, cut a 22½-inch-wide lengthwise strip and a 15½-inch-wide lengthwise strip from the long piece.

Cut your time in half when cutting reverse pieces for appliqué. Fold your fabric in half with wrong sides together, trace around your template, and cut out the two layers at once. You will automatically have one piece that is the reverse.

• For the background triangles, cut the 15⅞-inch-wide muslin strips into 15⅞-inch squares. Cut each square in half diagonally, as shown in **Diagram 1.**

• For the basket block corner triangles, cut the 5⅞-inch-wide tan strips into 5⅞-inch squares.

Cut six squares for the twin-size quilt and ten squares for the queen size. Cut each square in half diagonally.

• For the block sides, cut the $10^7/8$-inch-wide tan strips into $3 \times 10^7/8$-inch rectangles. You need 24 for the twin-size quilt and 40 for the queen-size quilt.

• For the squares for the baskets, cut the 3-inch-wide tan strips into twelve 3-inch squares for the twin-size quilt and twenty 3-inch squares for the queen-size quilt.

• For the border triangles, cut the $4^1/2$-inch-wide tan strips into fifty-four $4^1/2$-inch squares for either size quilt. Cut each square in half diagonally.

• For the basket triangles, cut the 25-inch-wide tan strips in half to make two 25×22-inch strips.

• For the setting squares, cut the $15^1/2$-inch-wide dark pink *lengthwise* strip into $15^1/2$-inch squares.

• For the side setting triangles, cut the $22^1/2$-inch-wide dark pink *lengthwise* strip into $22^1/2$-inch squares. Cut each square in half diagonally.

• For the corner setting triangles, cut the $11^1/2$-inch-wide dark pink strip into two $11^1/2$-inch squares. Cut each square in half diagonally.

• For the border triangles, cut the $4^1/2$-inch-wide dark pink strips into fifty-four $4^1/2$-inch squares for either size quilt. Cut each square in half diagonally.

• For the triangles for the top row of the baskets and the basket bottoms, cut the $3^3/8$-inch-wide brown strips into $3^3/8$-inch squares. Cut each square in half diagonally.

• For the basket triangles, cut the 25-inch-wide brown strips in half to make two 25×22-inch strips.

• For the flower bases, cut the 3-inch green strips into 3-inch green squares. Cut each square in half diagonally both ways to make four triangles. You need one triangle for each blossom.

• For the stems, cut the 1-inch-wide green strips into 6-inch lengths. You need 12 stems for the twin-size quilt and 20 stems for the queen-size quilt.

Note: Cut one sample block before cutting all the fabric for the quilt. Piece the entire block and appliqué the lilies in place. When you are satisfied

with the block, then repeat the sequence, making the required number of blocks for your size quilt.

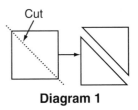

Diagram 1

Assembling the Baskets

Step 1. Five identical triangle squares are needed to complete each basket. The grid technique explained on page 106 in "Basket Basics" will help you to construct accurate triangle squares. Follow the instructions on that page, using a $3^3/8$-inch grid to make the number of triangle squares required for your quilt.

Step 2. Position five of the triangle squares with four $3^3/8$-inch basket fabric triangles and one 3-inch tan square, as shown in **Diagram 2A**.

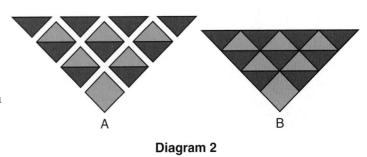

Diagram 2

Step 3. Sew the pieces together in diagonal rows, as shown. Press seams in opposite directions from row to row. Stitch the four resulting diagonal rows together. Press. See **2B**.

Step 4. Stack two $3 \times 10^7/8$-inch tan rectangles together, matching edges carefully. Align the 45 degree line on your plastic ruler with the edge of the rectangle, as shown in **Diagram 3** on page 90. Cut diagonally, making sure the angled cut is positioned to begin at the corner. The triangles cut from each rectangle won't be used in the basket, but they may come in handy for another project.

Note: If you are using a one-sided background fabric, the rectangles must be cut as mirror images. Stack each pair with wrong sides together, then trim as shown.

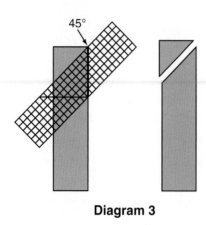

Diagram 3

Step 5. Sew two 3³/₈-inch basket fabric triangles to the untrimmed end of two rectangles, as shown in **Diagram 4.**

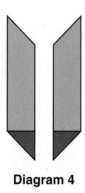

Diagram 4

Step 6. Sew the rectangle units to the partially assembled basket, as shown in **Diagram 5.** Align

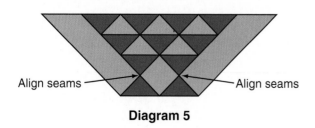

Align seams —   — Align seams

Diagram 5

the pieces where the seams meet, pressing seams in opposite directions before sewing. Press.

Step 7. Sew a 5⁷/₈-inch tan basket block corner triangle to the bottom of the basket, as shown in **Diagram 6,** completing the basket.

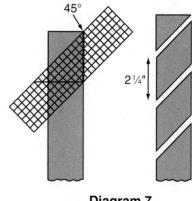

Diagram 6

ASSEMBLING THE BLOSSOMS

Step 1. The blossoms in the quilt shown are made from two different fabrics. Using a 2¹/₂-inch strip of petal fabric, align the 45 degree line of your ruler to a strip, as shown in **Diagram 7.** Make a diagonal cut, then align the ruler again to make another 45 degree cut 2¹/₄ inches away from the first cut. Cut two segments from each petal fabric for each blossom. You may want to cut only enough diamond segments to make one block before cutting all your fabric.

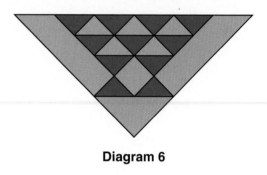

Diagram 7

Step 2. Sew the flower petals together in pairs, then sew the pairs together. Press seams in one direction. Center and sew a green triangle to the petals, as shown in **Diagram 8.**

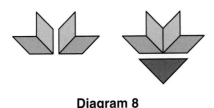

Diagram 8

Step 3. Repeat, making a total of three blossoms for each block.

APPLIQUÉING THE LILIES

Step 1. Prepare the blossoms for appliqué. We recommend that you try the interfacing method of appliqué for these blossoms. With this method, a piece of lightweight nonwoven interfacing is sewn to the front of the blossom, around its outer edges, with a standard ¼-inch seam allowance. After stitching all the way around the blossom, make a small slit in the interfacing only so you can turn the lily right side out to create an intact unit that is easy to appliqué in place. See page 109 in "Basket Basics" for details about this handy method.

— **Sew Easy** —

As an alternative to using interfacing for appliqué, try used fabric softener sheets from your dryer. Be sure to choose the flat white ones that look like interfacing and not the colored foam ones. They work just as well as interfacing and it's a great—and easy—way to recycle!

Step 2. Prepare the leaves and stems for appliqué using any of the methods described on pages 108–109 in "Basket Basics." You will need four leaves for each block—two using template A and four using template A reverse. Be sure to leave a sufficient raw edge of fabric at the inner point of each leaf so it can be tucked securely under the stem. The finished width of the stem should be ½ inch, with a length of approximately 5½ inches. You need one stem per block.

Step 3. Fold a 15⅞-inch muslin triangle in half once, as shown in **Diagram 9**, to find its center. Finger press to crease.

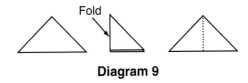

Fold

Diagram 9

Step 4. Open out the triangle and position the stem along the crease, making sure its bottom edge meets the long edge of the triangle. Pin or baste in place, then position the leaves, overlapping their inner edges with the stem where pieces meet, as shown in the **Block Diagram**. Place one of the blossoms at the top of the stem, positioning it so that the stem blends into the sepal, as shown in **Diagram 10**. Position the remaining two blos-

Block Diagram

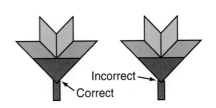

Incorrect

Correct

Diagram 10

soms on the background triangle, approximately ³/₄ inch above the raw edge of the triangle. The point of the sepal should line up with the intersection of triangles in the basket. Pin or baste the lilies in place. Appliqué all pieces to the triangle using the stitch of your choice.

Step 5. Sew the appliquéd triangle to the basket triangle to form a 15¹/₂-inch block. See the **Block Diagram** on page 91.

ASSEMBLING THE QUILT TOP

Notice that the quilt in the **Assembly Diagram** has all of its lilies pointing toward the left. If you'd like your lilies to point up, simply position your blocks in that direction before sewing the rows together.

Sew the lily blocks, setting squares, and setting triangles into diagonal rows, as shown in the **Assembly Diagram.** Press seams toward the setting squares and triangles. Sew the rows together. Press.

Assembly Diagram

Sew Easy
You may want to experiment with other layouts for your quilt. For example, for the queen-size quilt, have the center two rows point upward while each side row points inward. That way when the edges hang over the side of your bed, the lilies will look as if they're standing up in their baskets.

ADDING THE PIECED BORDER

The pieced borders are comprised of two long strips of alternating 4¹/₂-inch dark pink and tan triangles. The strips are then sewn together lengthwise to create a zigzag appearance, as shown in the **Quilt Diagram.** Handle the triangles carefully so you don't stretch their bias edges. The straight of grain is along their longest side.

Step 1. For the twin-size quilt, measure the length of the quilt top. For the queen size, measure the width of the quilt top. For either quilt, take the measurement through the center of the quilt rather than along the edge. This will be the finished length of each pieced border.

Step 2. Beginning with a dark pink triangle, sew pink and muslin triangles together, as shown in **Diagram 11,** until the strip is approximately 6¹/₂ inches longer than the required length. Repeat, beginning the second strip with a muslin triangle. Press the seams toward the pink triangles.

Diagram 11

Step 3. Sew the two strips together, as shown in **Diagram 12,** offsetting the strips so that the bases of pink triangles begin and end at the midpoint of the pink triangles in the adjoining strip.

Quilt Diagram

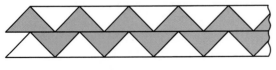

Diagram 12

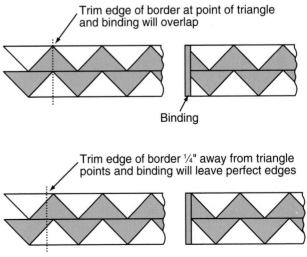

Trim edge of border at point of triangle and binding will overlap

Binding

Trim edge of border ¼" away from triangle points and binding will leave perfect edges

Diagram 13

Step 4. Cut the border to the length needed. To obtain a border that begins and ends at the mid-point of the zigzag design as the one shown, it may be necessary to ease in fullness of the border or quilt top to make it fit. When making a decision about beginning and ending points, remember that ¼ inch of each border end will be covered later by the binding. See **Diagram 13** for cutting the end of your border.

Step 5. Repeat Steps 2 through 4, making another pieced border.

Step 6. The Streak of Lightning border is attached to the sides of the twin-size quilt and the top and bottom of the queen-size quilt. Fold one pieced border in half crosswise to find its midpoint. Match the midpoint to the midpoint of the edge of the quilt and pin at that point, with right sides together. Match and pin the ends next, then pin along the entire edge, easing in fullness where necessary. Sew the border to the quilt using a ¹⁄₄-inch seam allowance. Press. Repeat, sewing the other border to the quilt, as shown in the **Quilt Diagram** on page 93.

QUILTING AND FINISHING

Step 1. Mark the quilt top for quilting. The quilt shown was outline quilted around each basket triangle and lily. The setting squares and triangles were quilted with a diamond-shape grid. Small hearts were quilted between the lily blossoms.

Step 2. Regardless of which quilt size you've chosen to make, the backing will have to be pieced.

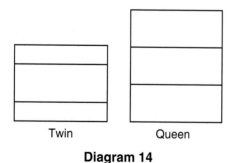

Twin   Queen

Diagram 14

To make the most efficient use of the yardage for both quilts, the back is pieced with the seams running horizontally, as shown in **Diagram 14.**

Step 3. For the twin-size quilt, divide the 5³⁄₈ yards of backing fabric into two equal segments, and trim the selvages. Cut one of the pieces in half lengthwise, and sew one half to each side of the full-width piece. Press the seams open.

Step 4. For the queen-size quilt, divide the 8 yards of backing fabric into three equal segments, and trim the selvages. Sew the pieces together along the long edges. Press the seams open.

Step 5. Layer the backing, batting, and quilt top. Baste the layers together, then quilt as desired.

Step 6. Referring to the directions on page 121 in "Quiltmaking Basics," make and attach double-fold binding. To calculate the amount of binding you will need for the quilt size you are making, add up the length of the four sides of the quilt and add 9 inches. The total is the approximate number of inches of binding you will need.

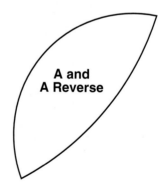

**A and
A Reverse**

ANTIQUE LILY BASKETS
Color Plan

Photocopy this page and use it to experiment with color schemes for your quilt.

Flower Baskets
Skill Level: *Easy*

Simple appliqué shapes with blanket-stitched edges create a folk art feeling in this charming 1930s-era twin-size quilt. The pastel colors and bubble-gum pink setting squares and borders are typical of the fabrics used during that period. Today's reproduction fabrics make it easy to re-create this cheerful quilt, which was obtained from an estate in Enid, Oklahoma.

BEFORE YOU BEGIN

The appliqué blocks in this quilt consist of simple flower, basket, and leaf shapes and embroidered flower stems. Refer to page 108 in "Basket Basics" and page 117 in "Quiltmaking Basics" for complete instructions about a variety of appliqué methods. While any method discussed can be used to make this quilt, we recommend you try one of the freezer paper techniques.

You will need to make templates for the individual appliqué pieces by tracing the flower, flower center, bud, leaf, and basket patterns on page 102. To mark the placement of the pieces and the stems onto the background block, you'll trace the basket, stem, flower, and flower center pattern as a unit, then transfer this pattern to the background block.

Quilt Sizes

	Twin (shown)	Queen
Finished Quilt Size	70" × 80"	90" × 100"
Finished Block Size	10"	10"
Number of Flower Basket Blocks	21	36

Materials

	Twin	Queen
Pink	3⅛ yards	4¼ yards
White	2¼ yards	3¾ yards
Green	½ yard	⅞ yard
Assorted prints	½ yard	⅝ yard
Assorted solids	½ yard	¾ yard
Yellow	⅜ yard	⅝ yard
Backing	5 yards	8⅝ yards
Batting	76" × 86"	96" × 106"
Binding	⅝ yard	¾ yard
Dark green embroidery floss		

NOTE: Yardages are based on 44/45-inch-wide fabrics that are at least 42 inches wide after preshrinking.

CHOOSING FABRICS

This quilt offers a great opportunity to work with some of the wonderful reproduction 1930s prints available today. For best results, use small amounts of a large assortment of fabrics. You can make every block different or make several combinations and repeat them throughout the quilt. Within each block, the flower is cut from a print; the flower center and buds match and are cut from a coordinating solid; and the basket and leaves are cut from solid fabrics.

Although the leaves in the original quilt are cut from a variety of green fabrics, we've listed only one green fabric in the Materials

97

Cutting Chart

Fabric	Used For	Strip Width	Number to Cut Twin	Number to Cut Queen
Pink	Setting squares	10½"	6	9
	Border	5½"	7	9
White	Background blocks	11"	7	12
Green	Leaves		84	144
Assorted prints	Flowers		21	36
Assorted solids	Flower centers		21	36
	Buds		42	72
Yellow	Baskets		21	36

list. You might choose to use a variety of green solids rather than just one. Or, for a different look, you might want to combine green solids with green prints.

To help develop your own unique color scheme for the quilt, photocopy the **Color Plan** on page 103, and use crayons or colored pencils to experiment with different color combinations.

The fabric requirements are listed as total yardages, but the flower, flower center, and bud pieces can also be cut from scraps. If you will be working with scraps, be sure you have at least the total amount of yardage listed. As an approximate guide to the size of the scrap needed, a flower can be cut from a 4½-inch print square, a flower center and two buds can be cut from a 4 × 6-inch solid rectangle, and four leaves can be cut from a 5½-inch solid or print square.

CUTTING

The measurements for the background blocks, setting squares, and borders include ¼-inch seam allowances. Referring to the Cutting Chart, cut the required number of strips in the width needed. Cut all strips across the fabric width (crosswise grain). For the setting squares, cut the 10½-inch-wide strips into 10½-inch squares. The background blocks are cut slightly oversize, then trimmed to 10½ inches after the appliqué is com-

plete. Cut the 11-inch-wide strips into 11-inch squares for background blocks. For the appliqué pieces, first make templates for the individual pieces using the full-size patterns on page 102. See page 116 in "Quiltmaking Basics" for details on making and using templates. Referring to the Cutting Chart, cut the number of pieces of each pattern required. Be sure to add seam allowances when cutting the pieces from fabric.

Note: Cut and stitch one sample block before cutting all the fabric for the quilt.

MAKING THE APPLIQUÉ BLOCKS

This quilt is made up of Flower Basket appliqué blocks, as illustrated in the **Block Diagram**, alternating with solid setting squares. Read through the general directions on page 108 in "Basket Basics" and on page 117 in "Quiltmaking Basics," then select an appliqué technique.

Block Diagram

Step 1. To help you position the appliqué pieces accurately, fold and crease a background square, creating guidelines. Fold a square in half vertically, then horizontally, and finger press. Then fold the square on both diagonals, finger pressing after each fold, as shown in **Diagram 1.** The creases formed will help you position the pieces.

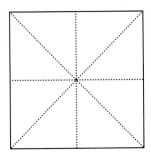

Diagram 1

Step 2. With a pencil, lightly mark the position of the basket, flower, and stems on the background block. To do this, trace the pattern on page 102 onto a large piece of tracing paper, then darken the lines with a permanent marker. Place the background block over the pattern, positioning the straight stem along the center crease of the fabric, as shown in **Diagram 2.** Lightly mark the pattern on the background block.

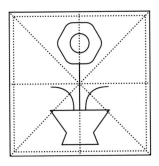

Diagram 2

Step 3. Prepare the following appliqué pieces: one print flower, one solid flower center, two solid buds that match the flower center, four solid leaves, and one solid basket. Pin the appliqué

— Sew Easy —

You can transfer the pattern easily using a hot-iron transfer pen. Trace the pattern onto tracing paper with the pen, then iron it onto the background block. Make sure the lines are thin, especially for the flower stems. The lines on the appliqué pieces will be covered with fabric, but since the stems will be embroidered, they must be thin in order to be invisible in the finished block.

Before ironing, double-check the position of the pattern to make sure it's centered correctly. One tracing can often be used several times. When the transfer fades, re-ink the lines, being careful to follow the original image.

pieces to the background square, placing the basket and flower on top of the marked guidelines and referring to the **Block Diagram** for correct placement of the leaves and buds. The flower center is the only shape that overlaps another; place it at the center of the flower.

Step 4. When you are satisfied that all of the pieces are in their proper positions, use two or three strands of green floss to embroider a running stitch for each stem line. Begin and end the embroidery so that the ends will be covered by the appliqué pieces when the block is complete.

Step 5. Appliqué the shapes to the background block using the technique of your choice. In the quilt shown, the quiltmaker appliquéd the pieces to the background using contrasting embroidery floss and a bold outline stitch.

Step 6. Repeat, making the required number of blocks for the quilt size you are making.

ASSEMBLING THE QUILT TOP

Step 1. Use a design wall or other flat surface to lay out the appliqué blocks and setting squares.

Sew Easy

To reduce bulk and make quilting easier, carefully trim the excess fabric from behind the flower appliqué. Turn the block over and gently lift the background fabric away from the appliqué. Make a small snip in the background fabric with your scissors, then cut away the fabric to within ¼ inch of the stitch line. Be sure to leave the ¼-inch seam allowance intact.

Refer to the appropriate quilt diagram for the correct layout for your quilt.

Step 2. Sew the blocks into rows, pressing the seam allowances in opposite directions from row to row. Join the rows, matching seams carefully. Press.

ADDING THE BORDERS

Step 1. Sew the 5½-inch-wide border strips together end to end, making four long borders. For the twin-size quilt, you will need two strips each for the side borders and one and a half strips each for the top and bottom borders. For the queen-size quilt, you will need two and a half strips each for the side borders and two strips each for the top and bottom borders.

Step 2. Measure the width of the quilt, taking the measurement through the horizontal center rather than along the edge. Trim the top and bottom borders to this exact length. Fold one strip in half crosswise and crease. Unfold it and position it right side down along one end of the quilt, with the crease at the vertical midpoint. Pin at the midpoint and ends first, then across the width of the entire quilt, easing in fullness if necessary. Sew the border to the quilt, using a ¼-inch seam allowance. Repeat on the opposite end of the quilt.

Step 3. Measure the length of the quilt, taking the measurement through the vertical center and including the top and bottom borders. Trim the

two side borders to this exact length. Fold one of the strips in half crosswise and crease. Unfold it and position it right side down along one side of the quilt, matching the crease to the horizontal midpoint. Pin at the midpoint and ends first, then along the entire length of the quilt, easing in fullness if necessary. Stitch, using a ¼-inch seam allowance. Repeat on the opposite side of the quilt.

Step 4. To round off the corners of the borders, as in the quilt shown, use a pencil to lightly draw around a plate or other circular object, as shown in **Diagram 3**. Be sure to position the plate in the same place on all four corners.

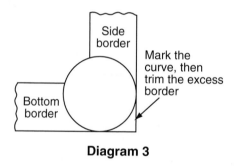

Diagram 3

Twin-Size Quilt Diagram

Queen-Size Quilt Diagram

QUILTING AND FINISHING

Step 1. Mark the quilt top for quilting. The flowers in the quilt shown were outline quilted, and a flower motif was quilted in the setting squares.

Step 2. Regardless of which quilt size you've chosen to make, the backing will have to be pieced. **Diagram 4** illustrates the two quilt backs. To make the backing for the twin-size quilt, cut the backing fabric crosswise into two equal pieces, and trim the selvages.

Step 3. Cut one piece in half lengthwise. Sew one half to each side of the full-width piece, as shown in the diagram. Press the seams open.

Step 4. To make the backing for the queen-size quilt, cut the backing fabric crosswise into three equal pieces, and trim the selvages. Sew the three pieces together along the long sides, as shown in the diagram, and press the seams open.

Step 5. Layer the quilt top, batting, and backing, and baste the layers together. Quilt as desired.

Step 6. Referring to the directions on page 121 in "Quiltmaking Basics," make and attach double-fold binding. To calculate the amount of binding needed for the quilt size you are making, add up the length of the four sides of the quilt and add 9 inches. The total is the approximate number of inches of binding you will need.

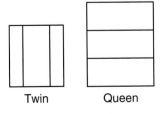

Twin   Queen

Diagram 4

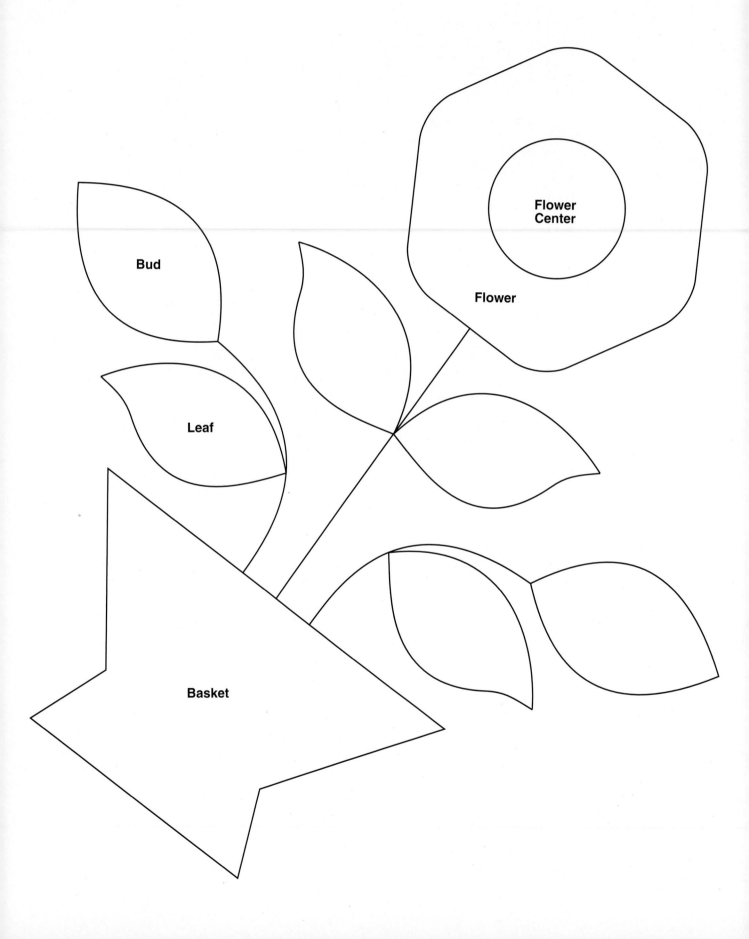

Flower Center

Flower

Bud

Leaf

Basket

Flower Baskets

Color Plan

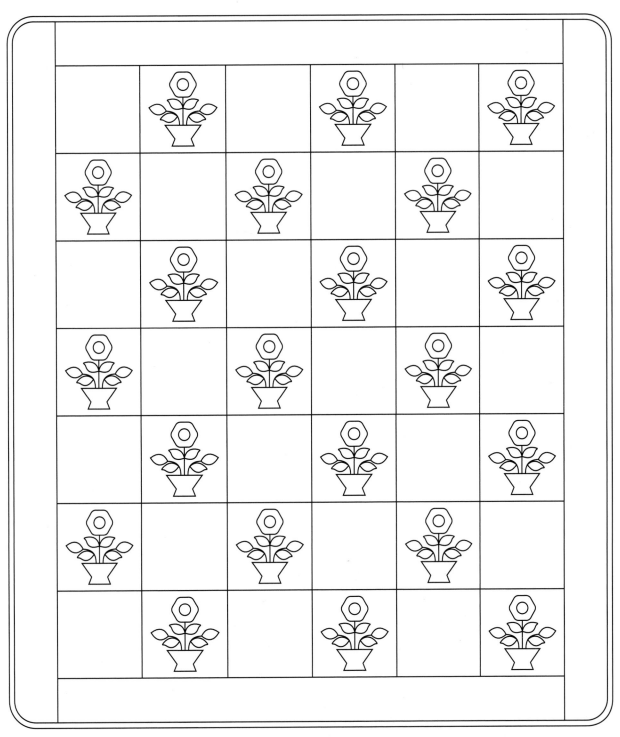

Photocopy this page and use it to experiment with color schemes for your quilt.

BASKET
BASICS

The projects in this book contain a variety of basket styles. Some are appliquéd, some are made from a single large triangle, and yet others are pieced from several triangle squares. In this section, you'll learn quick-and-easy techniques for all the cutting, piecing, and appliqué you'll need to make any of the baskets in the book. It's a good idea to read through this section before beginning any of the projects.

USING THE GRID METHOD TO MAKE TRIANGLE SQUARES

Many basket blocks are assembled from identical triangle squares. The grid method of construction allows you to assemble very accurate blocks much more quickly than you could using the traditional method of sewing together individual triangles.

With this method, two pieces of fabric are cut oversize, placed right sides together, then marked, sewn, and cut apart into individual triangle squares. The technique requires careful marking and sewing, but it produces multiples of identical triangle squares and allows you to avoid working with bias edges. It is an especially useful method when working with very small squares.

The grid from the Antique Lily Baskets project on page 86 is used as an example here to demonstrate the technique.

Step 1. To determine the correct size to cut the fabric, you must know the size of the squares in the grid and the number of squares you wish to make. These two important points are given in the directions for each project. The size of the squares is equal to the finished size of the triangle squares, plus $^7/_8$ inch. Each square in the grid will result in two triangle squares. In this example, the size of the squares is $3^3/_8$ inches, and the number of squares you need to make is 30 (resulting in 60 triangle squares, enough to make the twin-size quilt).

A grid of five squares by six squares will yield 30 squares and requires a $17^1/_2 \times 21$-inch piece of fabric. Since it's a good idea to allow a little extra

room on each side of the grid, cut two pieces of 22×25-inch fabric.

Step 2. Working on the wrong side of the lighter fabric, use a pencil or permanent marker to draw a grid of squares, as shown in **Diagram 1A**. Draw the grid at least $^1/_2$ inch in from the raw edges of the fabric. Referring to **1B**, carefully draw a diagonal line through each square in the grid.

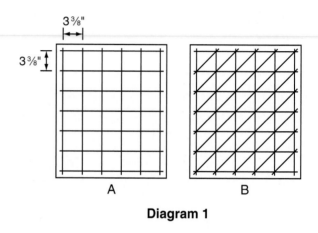

Diagram 1

Sew Easy

To make sure that your diagonal lines intersect the corners of the squares exactly, place the point of the marker at the corner first, then slide the edge of the ruler up against the pen point. You may find that a ball-point pen won't drag on the fabric as a pencil or other marker might.

Step 3. Position the marked fabric right sides together with the second piece of fabric. Using a $^1/_4$-inch seam allowance, stitch along both sides of the diagonal lines, as shown in **Diagram 2**. Use the edge of your presser foot as a $^1/_4$-inch guide, or draw a line $^1/_4$ inch from each side of the diagonal line.

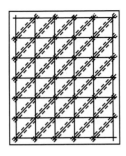

Diagram 2

Step 4. Use a rotary cutter and ruler to cut the grid apart. Cut on all the marked lines, as indicated in **Diagram 3A.** Carefully press the triangle squares open, pressing each seam toward the darker fabric. Trim off the triangle points at the seam ends, as shown in **3B.** Continue marking and cutting triangle squares until you have made the number required for the quilt you are making.

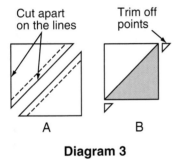

Cut apart on the lines   Trim off points

A   B

Diagram 3

SUPPLIES FOR APPLIQUÉ

- **Scissors:** You will need a very sharp pair of fabric scissors that cut all the way to the tips. You'll also need a pair of paper or utility scissors for cutting templates.
- **Templates:** You will need template material such as posterboard or template plastic to make templates for appliqué shapes. See page 116 in "Quiltmaking Basics" for information about making templates.
- **Thread:** Unless you choose to appliqué your block with decorative stitches, use a fine thread that matches the color of the piece being appliquéd. Silk thread glides easily through fabric and is almost invisible in the finished piece.
- **Needles:** For best results, use sharps or milliner's needles for hand appliqué.

PREPARING FOR APPLIQUÉ

Fabric Grain

Tradition says that the grain of pieces to be appliquéd should run in the same direction as the grain of the background they will be sewn onto. However, you may find it easier to fold under the seams of some shapes if they are cut on the bias, particularly those with deep inside curves. Another reason for breaking with tradition is that you may want to target a specific design in the fabric to use for a particular shape. If this means you need to cut on the bias, go ahead and do so.

Background Fabric

You may find it helpful to trace the entire design onto the background fabric before you begin, especially when assembling complex designs. Trace around individual templates to create a full-size block on paper, then use a light table or dressmaker's carbon to transfer the pattern onto the right side of your background fabric. For quick reference, record the color of each piece and its order in the design on your paper guide. If you decide to trace the appliqué shapes onto your background fabric, do so lightly and be sure that your appliqué pieces cover the markings.

To help you center the design more easily on the background, lightly press in some guidelines. To find the center of your fabric, fold it in half diagonally, then finger press. Unfold it and repeat on the other diagonal. Fold and finger press along the horizontal and vertical centers of the square, too. This procedure divides a square into eight equal segments, as shown in **Diagram 4,** making it simple to center the design and place all the elements evenly around the block.

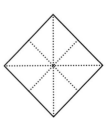

Diagram 4

CHOOSING AN APPLIQUÉ METHOD

Several of the most popular appliqué methods are described here. In addition to this discussion, see page 118 in "Quiltmaking Basics" for a description of needle-turn appliqué. You may find that a combination of methods will work best within the same block, depending on the individual shapes involved. We suggest that you experiment with each of these techniques to see which best suits your sewing style.

Sew Easy

Here are a few extra pointers for needle-turn appliqué, which is described on page 118 in "Quiltmaking Basics."

- Clip inner points and curves before sewing for a neater finished edge. Make a perpendicular cut into an inner point almost to the turn line. Make small V-shape cuts on inner curves, again almost to the turn line. Make as many cuts as necessary to help you achieve a smooth fold. Take a few extra appliqué stitches at cuts to reinforce fabric.
- Turn under points by cutting off the tip slightly. Fold the remaining seam allowance under to the turn line. Next, turn under the seam allowance on one side of the point, then the other. To achieve a sharp point and smooth seam, it may be necessary to trim excess fabric at the folds as you work.
- Edges of appliqué shapes that will be overlapped by another piece may be left unfinished.

Freezer Paper Appliqué Method 1

Freezer paper can help make many appliqué projects much easier. You will find plain white freezer paper at the grocery store, or you can purchase gridded freezer paper at quilt shops.

Step 1. Use a template to draw your patterns onto the dull (nonwaxy) side of freezer paper.

Step 2. Cut out the shapes on the line. Do not add a seam allowance.

Step 3. Use a medium to hot, dry iron to press the shiny (waxy) side of the shapes onto the right side of your fabric. The iron will soften the paper's coating, adhering it to your fabric.

Step 4. Cut out the shapes from fabric, leaving a $1/4$- to $3/8$-inch seam allowance around all edges of each template.

Step 5. Peel away the freezer paper, and center it with the waxy side up on the reverse of your fabric piece. Use the iron again, but this time press your seam allowance over the template. The waxy coating will again soften and hold your seam in place. This method eliminates basting, but you will still need to clip curves and points.

Sew Quick

A clean, hot-glue gun (*without* a glue stick) makes a handy iron for freezer paper appliqué. Its tip is just the right size to press seam allowances onto freezer paper, and it is easy to handle, helping you avoid burning your fingers.

Step 6. Appliqué the pieces to the block, then make a small slit in the background fabric and use a pair of tweezers to remove the freezer paper.

Freezer Paper Appliqué Method 2

Follow Steps 1 through 4 under "Freezer Paper Appliqué Method 1." Leaving the freezer paper adhered to the right side of your fabric, pin the piece to the background fabric. As you stitch the appliqué to the background, turn under the seam allowance along the edge of the freezer paper. Use the edge of the paper as a guide for the fold of your fabric. After your appliqué is stitched in place, gently peel off the freezer paper.

— Sew Easy

If you prefer to have appliqué edges pressed in position before beginning to stitch, hold them in place with spray starch. Spray a small amount of starch into a modest-size container, such as a plastic margarine tub. Use a cotton swab or small brush to paint the spray starch onto the seam allowance, concentrating it on the line where the actual turn will be. Press under the damp edges of the fabric with a medium-hot iron, allowing the edge of the freezer paper to guide you. The starch will hold the seam allowance in place while you hand stitch the appliqué in place.

Interfacing Appliqué Method

Nonwoven, nonfusible interfacing can be used to achieve perfect edges on appliqué shapes. You can also use clothes dryer fabric sheets that have been run through a dryer cycle to replace the interfacing. (Be sure to use only the stiff white sheets, not the colored foam types.)

Step 1. Trace around a template onto the interfacing or used dryer sheet. Cut out the shape, leaving an approximately 1/4-inch seam allowance on all sides.

Step 2. Place the wrong side of the cutout shape against the wrong side of the appliqué

fabric, then machine sew the two together directly on the traced line. Use a slightly smaller than normal straight stitch. Sew completely around the piece. Trim the seam allowance slightly, clipping into curves where necessary. Trim excess fabric away from points, too.

Step 3. Make a small slit in the center of the interfacing or dryer sheet. Do not cut too close to the stitching. Insert tweezers into the opening, grab the fabric, and pull it through the opening, turning the entire piece right side out. Run a blunt-edge tool, such as one used for stuffing dolls, along the seam inside the shape to eliminate puckers. Don't use the points of your scissors for this or you will likely end up with a hole in the fabric. Press the piece, then it's ready for appliqué.

— Sew Easy

Here's an easy way to make appliqué circles for flower centers. Cut a circle of the finished size from cardboard, an index card, or stiff template plastic. Cut a fabric circle approximately 3/8 inch larger than your template. Run basting stitches around the outer edge of the circle, slightly inside the seam allowance. Center the template on the wrong side of the fabric circle, then gather the basting stitches. Pull the seam allowance around the template, as shown. Smooth and press the fabric, then remove the paper. If any tucks remain, smooth them with your needle as you appliqué the piece to the background.

Cardboard

TRIMMING EXCESS FABRIC

If your design has many layers, it may be bulky in places, making it difficult to hand quilt those areas of the block. If you like, use very sharp scissors to carefully cut away extra layers. Working from the back of the block, cut away one layer at a time, being careful not to disturb the layer of fabric at the front of your block. This trimming also comes in handy when a dark background shows through a lighter appliquéd piece.

MAKING BIAS HANDLES AND VINES

Many of the baskets in this book have appliquéd bias strips for handles, since they bend so easily into graceful curves. Follow these steps to make bias strips for handles or vines.

Step 1. Use a rotary-cutting ruler to mark a 45 degree line on the handle fabric, as shown in **Diagram 5.**

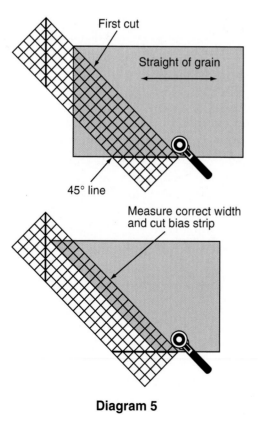

Diagram 5

Step 2. Cut bias strips parallel to the marked line, as shown. Each strip will be folded into thirds before being appliquéd, so multiply your desired finished width by 3, add approximately $^{1}/_{4}$ inch to that figure, and cut. For example, if the basket you are making requires a handle that has a finished width of $^{3}/_{4}$ inch, your bias strips should measure $2^{1}/_{2}$ inches.

Step 3. Fold each strip into thirds, as shown in **Diagram 6.** Make sure the raw edges will be concealed by the folded edges. Press carefully.

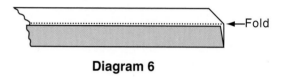

Diagram 6

Step 4. Curve the handle into position on the triangular portion of your block, as shown in **Diagram 7** (or in the quilt layout drawing for your pattern). Begin and end the strip at the bottom edge of the triangle. Baste or pin the handle in place, then appliqué it to the triangle, beginning with the inner curve. The raw edges at the ends of the handle will disappear when the basket top is sewn to the basket bottom.

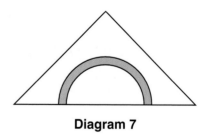

Diagram 7

USING BIAS BARS

Using a bias bar is particularly helpful when you need long, narrow stems or vines. Bias bars, which are sold in sets of several widths, are made to withstand the heat of an iron.

Step 1. Cut a bias strip, as shown in **Diagram 5**. The chart below lists cut widths for three sizes of bias strips. (Note that these widths apply only to strips cut for bias bars and not for strips meant to be folded into thirds, as described previously.)

Finished Width	Cut Width
1/8 inch	7/8 inch
1/4 inch	1 1/8 inches
3/8 inch	1 3/8 inches

Step 2. Fold the strip in half lengthwise, with *wrong* sides together. Press lightly to hold the edges of the fabric together as you stitch. To avoid stretching, do not move the iron back and forth—use an up-and-down motion. Sew the raw edges together using a standard 1/4-inch seam allowance. Trim the seam allowance to approximately 1/8 inch.

Step 3. Insert a bias bar of the correct width into the tube you've just created, turning the tube slightly to center the seam along the flat edge of the bar. Press the seam allowance to one side, dampening the fabric with water or a bit of starch to achieve crisp edges. Trim the seam allowance a bit more if it is too bulky.

Step 4. Flip the tube over, and check to be sure that the seam will be hidden when the bias is appliquéd to the quilt. When you are satisfied with the appearance, press the top side of the tube and remove the bias bar. If your vines are particularly long, you will have to slide the bias bar along the inside of the fabric tube to press the entire length before removing the bar.

EMBROIDERY BASICS

The Bluebirds of Happiness quilt on page 24 uses embroidery stitches to embellish the flowers in each basket. Three of the basic stitches used are the French knot, chain stitch, and outline stitch, as shown **Diagram 8.**

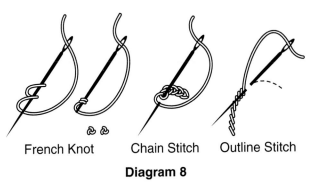

French Knot   Chain Stitch   Outline Stitch

Diagram 8

Sew Easy

Several of the quilts in this book feature flowers, including the Carolina Lily Medallion on page 42, Bluebirds of Happiness on page 24, and Flower Baskets on page 96. Here's an easy way to fill the other basket blocks with flowers, too. Simply choose a floral quilting design to stitch in the open space between the basket and the basket handle. For inspiration, take a look at some of the floral appliqué shapes in this book or page through a child's coloring book. You'll add a subtle touch that will fill your home with flowers year-round!

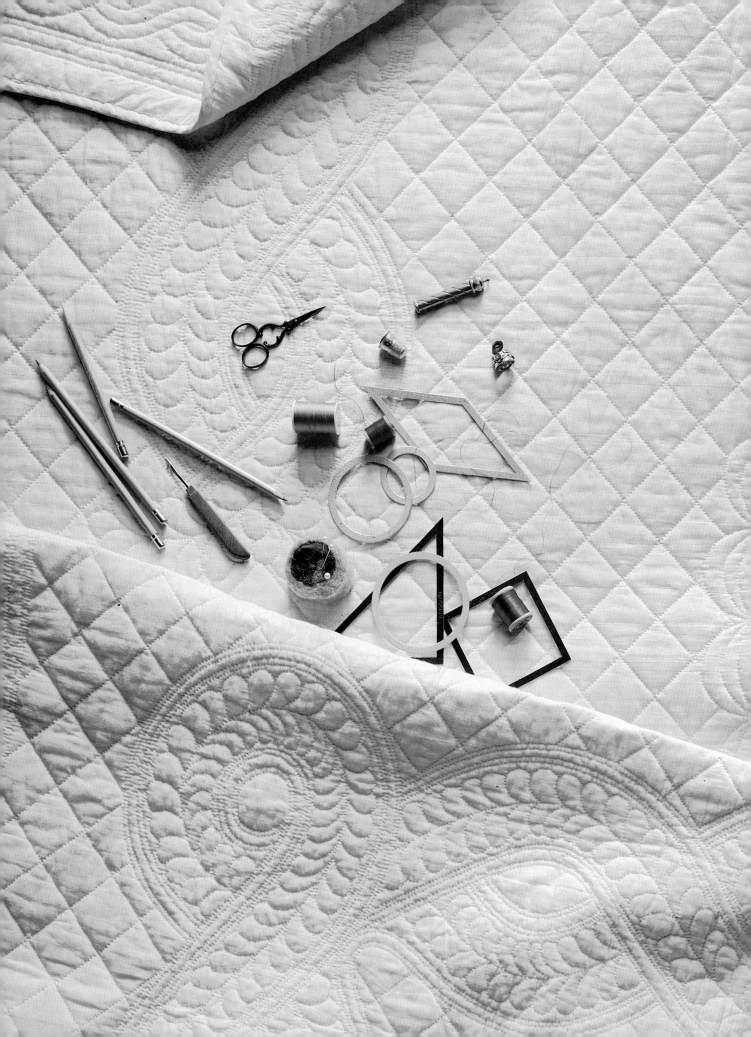

QUILTMAKING
BASICS

edge. Trace around the template onto the fabric, then add inner lines by eye.

LAYERING AND BASTING

Carefully preparing the quilt top, batting, and backing will ensure that the finished quilt will lie flat and smooth. Place the backing wrong side up on a large table or clean floor. Center the batting on the backing and smooth out any wrinkles. Center the quilt top right side up on the batting; smooth it out and remove any loose threads.

If you plan to hand quilt, baste the quilt with thread. Use a long darning needle and white thread. Baste outward from the center of the quilt in a grid of horizontal and vertical rows approximately 4 inches apart.

If you plan to machine quilt, baste with safety pins. Thread basting does not hold the layers securely enough during machine quilting, plus the thread is more difficult to remove when quilting is completed. Use rustproof nickel-plated brass safety pins in size #0, pinning from the center of the quilt out approximately every 3 inches.

HAND QUILTING

For best results, use a hoop or a frame to hold the quilt layers taut and smooth during quilting. Work with one hand on top of the quilt and the other hand underneath, guiding the needle. Don't worry about the size of your stitches in the beginning; concentrate on making them even, and they will get smaller over time.

Getting started: Thread a needle with quilting thread and knot the end. Insert the needle through the quilt top and batting about 1 inch away from where you will begin stitching. Bring the needle to the surface in position to make the first stitch. Gently tug on the thread to pop the knot through the quilt top and bury it in the batting.

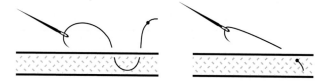

Taking the stitches: Insert the needle through the three layers of the quilt. When you feel the tip of the needle with your underneath finger, gently guide it back up through the quilt. When the needle comes through the top of the quilt, press your thimble on the end with the eye to guide it down again through the quilt layers. Continue to quilt in this manner, taking two or three small running stitches at a time.

Ending a line of stitching: Bring the needle to the top of the quilt just past the last stitch. Make a knot at the surface by bringing the needle under the thread where it comes out of the fabric and up through the loop of thread it creates. Repeat this knot and insert the needle into the hole where the thread comes out of the fabric. Run the needle inside the batting for an inch and bring it back to the surface. Tug gently on the thread to pop the knot into the batting layer. Clip the thread.

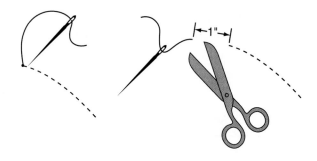

MACHINE QUILTING

For best results when doing machine-guided quilting, use a walking foot (also called an even feed foot) on your sewing machine. For free-motion quilting, use a darning or machine-embroidery foot.

Use thread to match the fabric colors, or use clear nylon thread in the top of the machine and a white or colored thread in the bobbin. To secure the thread at the beginning of a line of stitches, adjust the stitch length on your machine to make several very short stitches, then gradually increase to the regular stitch length. As you near the end of the line, gradually reduce the stitch length so that the last few stitches are very short.

For machine-guided quilting, keep the feed dogs up and move all three layers as smoothly as you can under the needle. To turn a corner in a quilting design, stop with the needle inserted in the fabric, raise the foot, pivot the quilt, lower the foot, and continue stitching.

For free-motion quilting, disengage the feed dogs so you can manipulate the quilt freely as you stitch. Guide the quilt under the needle with both hands, coordinating the speed of the needle with the movement of the quilt to create stitches of consistent length.

MAKING AND ATTACHING BINDING

Double-fold binding, which is also called French-fold binding, can be made from either straight-grain or bias strips. To make double-fold binding, cut strips of fabric four times the finished width of the binding, plus seam allowance. In general, cut strips 2 inches wide for quilts with thin batting and 2¼ inches wide for quilts with thicker batting.

Making Straight-Grain Binding

To make straight-grain binding, cut crosswise strips from the binding fabric in the desired width. Sew them together end to end with diagonal seams.

Place the strips with right sides together so that each strip is set in ¼ inch from the end of the other strip. Sew a diagonal seam and trim the excess fabric, leaving a ¼-inch seam allowance.

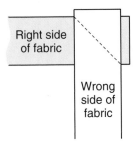

Making Continuous Bias Binding

Bias binding can be cut in one long strip from a square of fabric that has been cut apart and resewn into a tube. To estimate the number of inches of binding a particular square will produce, use this formula:

Multiply the length of one side by the length of another side, and divide the result by the width of binding you want. Using a 30-inch square and 2¼-inch binding as an example: 30 × 30 = 900 ÷ 2¼ = 400 inches of binding.

Step 1: To make bias binding, cut a square in half diagonally to get two triangles. Place the two triangles right sides together as shown and sew with a ¼-inch seam. Open out the two pieces and press the seam open.

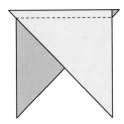

Step 2: Mark cutting lines on the wrong side of the fabric in the desired binding width. Mark the lines parallel to the bias edges.

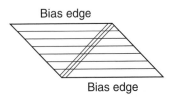

Step 3: Fold the fabric with right sides together, bringing the two nonbias edges together and offsetting them by one strip width (shown at the top of page 122). Pin the edges together, creating a tube, and sew with a ¼-inch seam. Press the seam open.

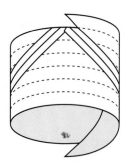

Step 4: Cut on the marked lines, turning the tube to cut one long bias strip.

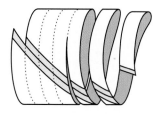

Attaching the Binding

Trim excess batting and backing even with the quilt top. For double-fold binding, fold the long binding strip in half lengthwise, wrong sides together, and press. Beginning in the middle of a side, not in a corner, place the strip right sides together with the quilt top, align the raw edges, and pin.

Step 1: Fold over approximately 1 inch at the beginning of the strip and begin stitching ½ inch from the fold. Sew the binding to the quilt, using a ¼-inch seam and stitching through all layers.

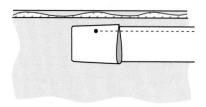

Step 2: As you approach a corner, stop stitching ¼ inch from the raw edge of the corner. Backstitch and remove the quilt from the machine. Fold the binding strip up at a 45 degree angle, as shown in the following diagram on the left. Fold the strip back down so there is a fold at the upper

edge, as shown on the right. Begin sewing at the top edge of the quilt, continuing to the next corner. Miter all four corners in this manner.

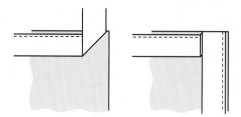

Step 3: To finish the binding seam, overlap the folded-back beginning section with the ending section. Stitch across the fold, allowing the end to extend approximately ½ inch beyond the beginning.

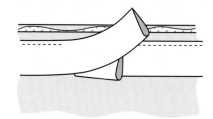

Step 4: Turn the binding to the back of the quilt and blindstitch the folded edge in place, covering the machine stitches with the folded edge. Fold in the adjacent sides on the back and take several stitches in the miter. In the same way, add several stitches to the miters on the front.

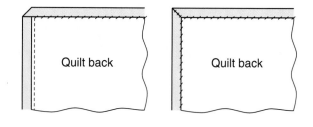

SIGNING YOUR QUILT

Be sure to sign and date your finished quilt. Your finishing touch can be a simple signature in permanent ink or an elaborate inked or embroidered label. Add any other pertinent details that can help family members or quilt collectors 100 years from now understand what went into your labor of love.